BANKING AND CHARITY IN SIXTEENTH-CENTURY ITALY

The Holy Monte di Pietà of Rome (1539–84)

Banking and Charity in Sixteenth-Century Italy

The Holy Monte di Pietà of Rome (1539–84)

FEDERICO ARCELLI

UPFRONT PUBLISHING
LEICESTERSHIRE

Banking and Charity in Sixteenth-Century Italy
Copyright © Federico Arcelli 2003

All rights reserved

No part of this book may be reproduced in any form by
photocopying or by any electronic or mechanical means,
including information storage or retrieval systems,
without permission in writing from both the copyright
owner and the publisher of this book.

ISBN 1-84426-102-6

First published 2003 by
UPFRONT PUBLISHING LTD
Leicestershire

Typeset in Bembo by
Bookcraft Ltd, Stroud, Gloucestershire
Printed by Lightning Source

To my beloved wife Paola

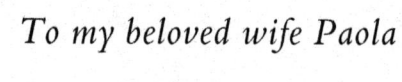

CONTENTS

Preface ix

Sources xi

Introduction xv
The origins of the *monti di pietà* xv
The Franciscans' objective xvi
Notes . . . . *xvii*

I THE HISTORICAL SETTING

**Credit in the fourteenth to sixteenth centuries:
  the rules of the game** 1
Credit and merchants in the fourteenth to sixteenth centuries 1
The interests affected by the *monti di pietà* 2
Avoidance of the rules on usury:
  do constraints stimulate innovation? 4
The *monti di pietà*: between faith and the market. 5
Rome in the sixteenth century: an economic and political centre 8
Credit and business in the shadow of the papal court 9
The local economy. 10
The papal administration 11

The Monte's evolving role 11
The early years 11
The turning point and after 13
Notes *14*

II THE MONTE DI PIETÀ OF ROME AS AN ECONOMIC AGENCY

The Monte's operations. 21
The activities performed by the Monte 21
Interests on deposits and reimbursement of expenses on loans. 22
Fund-raising 23
The link with government. 26
The accounts of the Deposit Bank in its first year of activity 26
Other activities 28
Buildings 32

Banking and Charity in Sixteenth-Century Italy

Lending and pawnbroking: scope and procedures 34
The Monte's credit activity, 1539–84 34
Growth and credit risk. 35
Interest, lending and collateral 38

Administrative control and managerial powers 42
The organisational structure of administration. 42
The first meetings of the congregation 44
The effect of the merger with the Company of San Bernardo. . . . 46
Further modifications up to the Statutes of 1581. 48

The salaries of the Monte's permanent employees. 50
Salary payments between 1541 and 1562 50

A case of public intervention in the economy. 57
The Monte di Pietà of Rome as an economic agency 57
The Monte's slow evolution into a state bank 58
Notes *62*

APPENDIX

Events and operations, 1539–84 71
The protectorate of Cardinal Francisco Quinones (1539–40): the
    founding of the Monte 71
The regency of Gaspare Contarini (July–November 1540) 72
The Monte during the protectorate of Rodolfo Pio di Carpi
    (1540–64): the transition from small charitable association
    to economic organisation. 73
The merger of the Ospedale Boemo 75
The merger with the Company of San Bernardo 77
Towards the first statutes 79
The final meetings of Pio di Carpi's protectorate 83
The protectorate of Charles Borromeo (1564–72) 84
The new statutes for the birth of an efficient credit organisation. 87

**From 1572 until the conferral of the
Deposit Bank in 1584**. 88
The protectorate of Cardinal Giulio Feltre della Rovere (1573–8) 88
The protectorates of Cardinals Francesco Alciati (1579–80)
    and Filippo Guastavillani (1580–7). 90
Notes *91*

Bibliography 101
Archive references 106

TABLES

Table I *Estimated operating expenses of the Monte di Pietà of Rome, 1540–50* 12

Table II *Annual interest payments and average interest rate on Rome public debt securities* 24

Table III *Deposits at the Monte di Pietà of Rome in its early years (1540–82)* 25

Table IV *Cumulative balances of deposits for judicial proceedings at the Monte di Pietà of Rome: first financial year (1 October 1584–30 September 1585)* 28

Table V *Payments and funds transfers between the Monte and third parties or customers, 1541–82* 29

Table VI *Total end-year stock of Roman public debt securities outstanding* 31

Table VII *Rent payments to Gian Pietro Crivelli for business offices of the Monte di Pietà of Rome, 1539–45* 32

Table VIII *Estimate of the Monte's total lending activity, 1539–84* 37

Table IX *Payments and funds transfers for administrative activity of the Monte, 1540–74* 46

Table X *Salaries paid, 1541* 52
Table XI *Salaries paid, 1542* 52
Table XII *Salaries paid, 1543* 53
Table XIII *Salaries paid, 1544* 54
Table XIV *Salaries paid, 1545* 54
Table XV *Salaries paid, 1546* 55
Table XVI *Salaries paid, 1547* 55
Table XVII *Salaries paid, 1559* 55
Table XVIII *Salaries paid, 1560* 56
Table XIX *Salaries paid, 1561* 56
Table XX *Salaries paid, 1562* 56

Table XXI *Offerings personally presented on 3 May 1552 by officers of guilds in Rome* 80

PREFACE

The combination of banking and welfare functions in a single institution would probably be labelled today as an overwhelmingly challenging task. By a paradox of history, just such a model, the *monti di pietà*, pawnbroking institutions that arose in Europe between the late 1400s and mid-1500s, sought to bring together solicitude for the poor and the needs of the economy, the objectives of politics and the resources of finance – all this with the explicit blessing (and implicit approval) of the Catholic Church, which continued to wield major influence in economic affairs despite the advance of Protestantism and the change in historical conditions.

This work begins with an account of what the *monti di pietà* represented in the historical period of their foundation. It then concentrates on the Monte di Pietà of Rome, which in the intention of its founders was to be *primus inter pares* and the model's crowning achievement. The aim is to shed light on a 'historical phenomenon' that influenced both the practical development of banks as financial institutions – as testified to by the fact that various *monti* survive today, though many of them have been merged into major commercial banks – and, more generally, the political vicissitudes of many Renaissance states. Equally important, the birth of the *monti di pietà* affected contemporary theological debate, above all on the question of usury, and conditioned relations, at least in financial matters, between the Catholic majority in southern and central Europe and the minorities who lived on commerce and trade, notably the Jews and certain Protestant communities. These issues have been studied under many perspectives. Here they are addressed from the specific viewpoint of the establishment of the Monte di Pietà of Rome, its evolution into a state agency of the apostolic administration and its impact on the Roman economy.

This monograph provides elements for a critical revision of some conventional judgements of the effects of usury on the economy under Church rule. Financial innovation by merchant bankers might be partly viewed as a consequence of the constraints imposed by doctrine. The text also reports a comment contained in Keynes' General Theory suggesting a new view of the rules of the game of credit in the fourteenth to sixteenth centuries. Many questions are raised in connection with the results acquired by historical research.

The text is a concise survey yet a comprehensive elaboration of material drawn from historical archives. It includes also original documents from the Vatican's 'secret archive' which are examined for the first time after centuries of neglect because up to now there was no access to such sources.

I am indebted in particular to Prof. Giuseppe Di Taranto (University of Naples), who helped and advised me through all this work. I am also grateful to Professors Dario Antiseri (LUISS – Guido Carli University, Rome), David Gowland (Derby University, UK), Marzio Achille Romani and Marco Cattini (Bocconi University, Milan), Ciro Manca ('La Sapienza' University, Rome), Luciano Palermo (LUISS – Guido Carli University, Rome) and Piero Bolchini (Ca' Foscari University, Venice), for their careful reading of a draft of the research and for their comments.

I would like to thank Prof Sergio Bastianel SJ, Dean of Theology at the Pontificia Università Gregoriana of Rome, for useful discussions on usury doctrine in the fourteenth to seventeenth centuries. I wish to remember also Franco Pisa, who gave me interesting sources and bibliography on local credit matters in the late fifteenth and sixteenth centuries, and Massimo Fornasari, who provided me with references and advice on the subject, and to the personnel of the Archives of the Banca di Roma, and, in particular, to Dr Michele Barbato, Dr Paolo Gaballo, Dr Fabio Del Giudice and Dr Alfredo d'Anchise. I shall award a special mention to Daniel Dichter, who helped me in the restructuring of the whole text and in the English translation of this work.

I remain, of course, solely responsible for what is written in the following pages.

SOURCES

The surviving archival documentation on the Sacro Monte di Pietà of Rome is incomplete and fragmentary. The material available for consultation is divided among four main repositories and a host of smaller collections. The bulk of the documentation is still preserved at the historical building at No. 33, Piazza Monte di Pietà in Rome, which served continuously as the Monte's headquarters from the early 1600s onwards.[1] The holdings include most of the ledgers, the originals of the principal papal bulls concerning the Monte and an enormous number of sundry documents regarding the institution's transactions and activities over the course of time. The archives of the Sacro Monte di Pietà of Rome at the Archives of the Banca di Roma (henceforth ASMP) are private holdings and accessible subject to authorisation; an inventory was only recently drawn up. Another group of documents regarding the Monte is kept at the State Archives of Rome (ASR), and a smaller one at the Archivio Segreto Vaticano (ASV). Other documents are to be found at various minor archives and in Paris.

The registers preserved at ASMP that were consulted constitute virtually all the surviving documentation on the Monte's early period of activity, running from its foundation to the conferral of the Deposit Bank (1584), an event that effectively marked the transformation of the Monte into a state agency of the apostolic administration. The documentation is predominantly descriptive,[2] providing information on the matters discussed in the meetings of the Monte's *congregazione*, a body roughly comparable to the board of directors, composed of the *deputati* (delegates) of the Company of the Monte. Unfortunately, nothing has come down to us of the Monte's general accounts and balance sheets for the period up to 1584. For our knowledge of the institution's financial and capital structure and of the flows of funds arising in the course of ordinary activity in those years, we have to rely primarily on the second part of Tome 20 of the *Decreti* (resolutions), which records the complete series of wage payments to permanent staff up to 1561, interspersed with the notation, probably serving as memoranda, of a number of financial transactions (deposits, trusts, funds transfers and payments of judicial expenses). Other quantitative information, above all the total number of pledge loans for the period under study, can be derived from the so-called *Nota del Gabrielli*.[3] In addition, fragmentary citations of accounting data are scattered here and there in the minutes of meetings of the congregation. These generally concern the ceiling on the value of loans per person and per transaction, and, occasionally, claims or deposits subject to litigation with third parties. These notes also refer to decisions concerning changes in staff wages and out-of-pocket expenses to be borne for the rental of buildings.

ASMP also has a series of documents that gather together the main bulls, edicts and notes regarding the Monte and its relations with the apostolic administration. These include the '*Registro di Bolle, Brevi e Decreti di Congregazione*', Tome I, containing, *inter alia*, the original of the institutive bull *Ad Sacram Beati Petri Sedem*,[4] and the '*Registro di Lettere Apostoliche ed Instromenti Diversi*'. In general, the documents available in ASMP are of interest principally for an analysis of the Monte's corporate and economic structure, but only at the risk of considerable approximation can they be used to build a picture of the institute's real impact on the Roman economy. The latter caveat holds mainly for the period up to the mid-1600s: account books summarising the institution's balance sheets from 1659 onwards are available, albeit with lacunae especially in the accounts of the Deposit Bank, for which the earliest surviving accounting records date from the nineteenth century.

The material kept by the State Archives of Rome (ASR) is a good deal thinner on the Monte's organisational structure but a bit more significant as regards the economic aspects of the institution's early years. It includes a nearly complete series of ledgers referring to the Monte's ordinary operating accounts from 1584 to the mid-1700s. These volumes, well preserved, are currently stored at the Archives' subsidiary premises. The series, of some interest, is rather difficult to interpret, since the style of the texts recalls the accounting records kept by merchants for their private companies. It is likely that the ledgers were drawn up by

Sources

employees of the merchants who held office at the Monte – as depositary or treasurer – and perhaps even by these merchants themselves. The records are very detailed and refer to individual loan or deposit transactions, occasionally grouped by type, date or the official, a *deputato* or a *provvisore*, who had authorised them. It should be borne in mind that it was standard practice, sanctioned by several resolutions of the congregation, never to lend against multiple pledges or to accept more than one pledge per person. Barring exceptions, this rules out the presence of multiple accounts, i.e. more than one transaction with the same counter-party, which are frequent in the books of the merchant companies. As a whole, the documentation at ASR is of some importance. If adequately exploited, it could provide information on the scale of the impact of the Monte's activity on the Roman economy, especially in the seventeenth century. However, its usefulness for the present study was limited, in the first place, because it does not reach back to before 1584 and, second, because the difficulty of accessing it and its scale (each ledger is between 500 and 800 pages long) precluded anything but random checks.

On the other hand, it is worth underscoring the importance of the documentation stored at ASV, especially the copy of the statutes[5]. The document in question is a printed copy of the 1581 version of the Monte's statutes, published during the protectorate of Cardinal Filippo Guastavillani (1580–7), which also contained a printed copy of the bull of 9 September 1539 founding the Monte.[6] Its importance lies chiefly in the fact that all the copies of statutes in the series available at ASMP are from later dates. The version drafted at the behest of the then Protector Charles Borromeo around 1565 has not come down to us, nor has the text proposed in 1557 by Cardinal Rodolfo Pio of Carpi, of which we have summary mention in Tome 30 of the *Decreti*. The statutes in ASV are therefore the official version closest in time to the historical text written for Borromeo and, to the best of my knowledge, the oldest existing copy of statutes of the Monte di Pietà of Rome excluding the text in the Vatican Library, which some identify with the Borromean version of 1565 but whose dating is problematic.[7] The rest of the documentation in ASV consists mainly of bulls, edicts and bills concerning the privileges of the Monte. It is of marginal usefulness for quantifying the institution's volume of business, but it does offer corroborating evidence of the decisions described in the minutes of the congregation.[8]

The material regarding the Monte in other archives and libraries relates to the period between the seventeenth and nineteenth centuries and is therefore not relevant for the purposes of this study.

For printed sources, I availed myself of the publications in the collection of ASMP, which keeps a copy of every work that in some way relates to the Monte. Among these, I made particular use of the two rather dated monographs by Donato Tamilia (1900) and by Mario Tosi (1936).[9] The latter, writing only months from the merger of the Monte into Cassa di Risparmio di Roma, expressed the hope that the centuries-old institution would shortly celebrate its fourth centenary 'amidst all the renewed flourishing and splendour of its refoundation'.[10] I also consulted works not available at ASMP as a result of helpful suggestions and advice, for which I am indebted.

INTRODUCTION

The origins of the *monti di pietà*

Monti di pietà arose in swift succession in many places in Italy beginning in the second half of the fifteenth century. The first was founded in Perugia, apparently in 1462, followed by a constellation: one in Milan, Bologna (1473), Ravenna (1492) and Naples (1539), several in the Marches (1400s), one in Siena (1472), still others[11] and finally one in Rome in 1539, following Naples. The historical impact of these institutions was considerable. Their very creation indirectly influenced local political conditions and their subsequent activity affected the credit market and artisanal production, in keeping with their founders' official intentions of ensuring the needy easy access to small loans.

In order to finance essential consumption at no 'mark-up', the *monti* were bound by special rules.[12] Combining welfare concerns and lending in a hybrid structure that was at once charitable institution and public agency dominated by the local authorities, the early *monti* were also designed by the Franciscans, their main promoters, as an instrument that would supplant Jewish moneylending.[13] This consideration was doubly important for the Monte di Pietà of Rome, which was meant to symbolise the success of the entire economic and social endeavour.

Credit in the late middle ages remains the subject of major debate. The most widely accepted hypothesis on the working of the medieval capital market has tended to distinguish between 'exchange' bankers, most of them Christians, and 'moneylenders', generally Jews specifically licensed by the local authorities.[14] This distinction implicitly acknowledges the teachings of the Church on the matter of usury.[15] It is also the consensus view that the Church, enjoying unique political status as the universally recognised ultimate source of authority[16] and commanding enormous economic power as a result of the payments connected with benefices and the relationships revolving around the temporal interests of the papacy, was able to impose valid rules in the realm of finance.[17] Nonetheless, the campaign that was launched in the second half of the fifteenth century with the establishment of *monti di pietà* appears less a reaffirmation of an unquestioned primacy than a last attempt to restore a rule-making power in the realm of economic activity that had begun to vacillate with the erosion of the Mediterranean's central position in the world market (owing not least to the Ottoman advance) and the growing malaise in a Europe soon to be divided by the Protestant Reformation.[18]

The Franciscans' objective

In emphasising that those in need had to be assisted free of charge, irrespective of all economic or market considerations, the Friars Minor in fact equated authorised loan banks with usurious lenders.[19] Behind this accusation was a not uncommon situation in which the civil authorities, at times with the assent of the Church (the exception confirming the rule), granted official licences (*condotte*) to non-Christians to engage in local lending. One of the motives of the Franciscans' campaign against local moneylenders was that the credit the latter advanced was possibly used to finance essential consumption rather than business ventures or activity.[20]

The Franciscan position implicitly rejected the concept of 'capital market', at least in a general form, for they asserted that any local credit granted as an advance for basic consumption to indigent or needy borrowers had to be strictly free of charge. Indeed, it could be said that this was the crux of the long debate between the Franciscans and the Dominicans and not the question of whether it was opportune to establish *monti di pietà* that would in practice be credit institutions, or the custom, dating from after the Fifth Lateran Council, of demanding reimbursement of expenses in order to support the *monti*.[21]

The Dominicans took a more rigid position than the Franciscans, arguing that any remuneration of a loan in and of itself constituted 'usury', regardless of the purpose of the loan or the form of the 'premium'. Strictly speaking, moreover, loans to indigents must not be loans but gifts made in the name of God (recalling Luke 6:35: '… *Mutuum date, nihil inde sperantes*…'). The Franciscans appeared at least formally to concur that any 'premium' or return on principal constituted usury, but their approach in practice aimed at paving the way for intervention in the credit market that would correct its main deviations from an orthodox vision. Paradoxically, their efforts, which led to the *monti di pietà*, resulted in theology adjusting to economic realities, as is evident in the question of reimbursement of expenses. Paradoxically again, the fact that most local moneylenders were Jews licensed by the competent authorities helped the Franciscans to win out over the more intransigent Dominicans. In a sense, the violence of the Franciscans' anti-Jewish preaching, hardly an example of Christian tolerance or of what nowadays we would be tempted to call the 'ecumenical spirit', can be seen as a device for attaining a broader objective: the establishment of an economic model more in keeping with the values of Christianity.

Evidence of the success of this endeavour is the diminishing role played by private banks in local credit in the 1500s, although this was also the product of other factors. Certainly, it is difficult to dispute the view, put forward by F Melis, that in the late 1500s the *monti* began to assume the basic function that had once been the prerogative of the private banks.[22] But in Rome and, I believe, many other places this transition was not automatic but grew out of the evolution into banks of institutions that had originally had very different features. Fornasari quite rightly remarks that this began to happen in the late sixteenth century.[23] In the dynamic setting of Rome, where the merchant companies, led by the Medici Bank, had figured prominently during the fifteenth century and throughout the sixteenth, the solid establishment of the Sacro Monte di Pietà towards the end of the sixteenth century represented a major change in local economic life. Beyond its importance as local history, however, an investigation of the birth and early period of activity of the Sacro Monte di Pietà of Rome is also an opportunity to observe the vicissitudes of the institution that was meant to crown an entire economic model.[24]

Notes

1 The meeting of the Monte's administrative board of 21 October 1603, chaired by Cardinal-Protector Pietro Aldobrandini (served 1602–21), nephew of Pope Clement VIII, approved the purchase of a building that had belonged to the Santacroce family and had then been owned by the Petrignanis. The building, remodelled and restructured, has remained the Monte's head office into the current century. In 1937 the Monte merged with Cassa di Risparmio di Roma. Thereafter the building hosted the institution's historical archives and its pawnbroking business, which continues today. The latter is now carried out directly by Banca di Roma SpA, the institution that succeeded to Cassa di Risparmio following the latter's merger with Banco di Santo Spirito in 1990 and the merger of the resulting institution, which retained the name of Banco di Santo Spirito, with Banco di Roma in 1992. The oldest component of today's Banca di Roma is the Monte, which was officially established on 9 September 1539 by Pope Paul III with the bull *Ad Sacram Beati Petri Sedem* . For a monograph study of the

Banking and Charity in Sixteenth-Century Italy

historic building at Piazza Monte di Pietà, see M. Carta, *Il Palazzo del Monte di Pietà di Roma*, in the series 'I palazzi della Banca di Roma', Rome, Arti grafiche f.lli Palombi, 1994.

2   The documentation consists in part of various volumes of the *'Registri dei Decreti di Congregazione del Sacro Monte di Pietà'*. I have made largest use of Tomes 39 (years 1540–66), 40 (1566–79) and 41 (1580–93). It also includes the *'Registri di Brevi, Instromenti e Decreti di Congregazione del S. Monte di Pietà dal 1540 al 1604 o meglio al 1626'* (bound in Tome 13) containing a summary of the volumes of the series of *Decreti* (resolutions) entitled *'Nota Decretorum Congregationis'*, years 1540–1604, which I have used mainly for cross-checking and comparisons relating to the years between 1540 and 1593, the period covered by the first three tomes of *decreti*.

3   ASMP, Tome 258. The full title is *Nota di libri e scritture che si trovano nell'archivio del Sacro Monte della Pietà, et appresso li officiali et ministri di detto Monte reviste et poste per ordine de' tempi dal Sig. Carlo Gabrielli, Deputato, come per decreto a dì 13 di Maggio 1603*.

4   ASMP, Tome I, c.24.

5   On the *Statuti*, see in particular F. Arcelli, *Gli Statuti del 1581 del Sacro Monte di Pietà di Roma*, Soveria Mannelli (CZ), Rubbettino, 1999.

6   ASV, *'Bolle per diverse Militie di Cavalieri per diversi collegij di Roma per il Monte di Pietà e per la S.ta Casa di Loreto'*, Armario IV, Tome 22, pp.486–506 (statutes of the Monte printed during the protectorate of Cardinal Guastavillani, 1581).

7   See D. Tamilia, *Il Sacro Monte di Pietà di Roma*, Rome, Forzani & c., 1900, pp.39–40. The text, at Biblioteca Apostolica Vaticana, Codice Vaticano Latino 6203, cc.150–69, bears no date. Although it plausibly may date from before the 1580s and actually be the Borromean text of 1565, the 1581 version reprinted here has the advantage of being datable with certainty.

8   The resolutions of the deputies of the congregation were not always followed by concrete action, owing to the interplay of tasks and responsibilities with other bodies of the apostolic administration. A formal notice or edict may prove that a given decision was actually translated into action.

9   M. Tosi, *Il Sacro Monte di Pietà di Roma e le sue Amministrazioni*, Rome, Ist. Pol. dello Stato, 1936.

10 Tosi, *op. cit.*, p.336.

11 G. Mira, 'Note sul Monte di Pietà di Perugia dalle origini alla seconda metà del XVI secolo', in *Archivi storici delle aziende di credito*, Rome, ABI – Associazione Bancaria Italiana, 1956, vol. I, pp.343–52; A. Cova, 'Banchi e monti pubblici in Milano nei secoli XVI e XVII', in *Banchi pubblici, banchi privati e monti di pietà nell'Europa preindustriale*, Proceedings of the conference held in Genoa, 1–6 Oct. 1990, Genoa, Società Ligure di Storia Patria, 1991; M. Fornasari, *Il Thesoro della città – Il Monte di Pietà e l'economia bolognese nei secoli XV ed XVI*, Bologna, Il Mulino, 1993, published in the series on economic and banking history, promoted by the Fondazione del Monte di Bologna e Ravenna; M. Fornasari, 'Il Monte di Pietà di Ravenna: storia di una istituzione sociale (1492–1939)', in M. Fornasari, P. Mita and M. Poli, *I cinquecento anni del Monte di Ravenna (1492–1992)*, Bologna, Il Mulino, 1992, published on behalf of the Fondazione del Monte di Bologna e Ravenna; L. De Rosa, 'Banchi pubblici, banchi privati e monti di pietà a Napoli nei secoli XVI e XVIII', in *Banchi pubblici, banchi privati e monti di pietà nell'Europa preindustriale, op. cit.*; V. Bonazzoli, 'Monti di Pietà e politica economica delle città delle Marche alla fine del '400', *ibid.*; M. Ciardini, *I banchieri ebrei in Firenze nel secolo XV e il monte di pietà fondato da Girolamo Savonarola – Appunti di storia economica con appendice di documenti*, Borgo San Lorenzo, 1907; reprinted Florence, 1970, doc. VI.

12 The pledge loan, the principal instrument used by the *monti*, was well-suited to the avowed principles of welfare. In the earliest period of the *monti* the grant of credit carried no charge, not even for 'repayment of expenses'. The loan was at short term (3–6 months, generally with the possibility of at least one renewal) and was secured by goods (valuables or furnishings) deemed upon acceptance to be of sufficient value to cover the risk of default by the debtor. Valuation was often left to the judgement of the official appraiser. The *monti* set strict limits on the amount of money that could be lent to any one customer, usually a relatively modest sum equivalent to one or two months' wages for a journeyman. They also limited the number of acceptable pledges, often to no more than one.

Notes to Introduction

13 G. Mira, 'Considerazioni sulla lotta dei Monti di Pietà contro il prestito ebraico', in *Scritti in memoria di Sally Mayer*, Milan, 1956, pp.199–205.

14 See M. Cassandro, 'Sulla storia economica degli Ebrei nei secoli XV–XVII. Problemi, orientamenti e prospettive, in *Studi in memoria di Mario Abrate*, Turin, 1986, vol. 1, pp.271–88, and M. Luzzati, 'Ruolo e funzioni dei banchi ebraici dell'Italia centro-settentrionale nei secoli XV e XVI', in *Banchi pubblici, banchi privati e monti di pietà nell'Europa preindustriale, op.cit.*

15 Salient moments of the theological debate on credit and usury are to be found, among others, in Thomas Aquinas, *Summa Theologiae*, vols. IV–XVII of *Opera Omnia*, Rome, 1882; Alexander of Hales, *Summa Theologica*, Florence, Quaracchi, 1924, vol. I; Abelard, 'Petri Abelardi Opera Theologica. Commentaria in Epistulam Pauli ad Romanos. Apologia contra Bernardum', in *Corpus Christianorum – continuatio mediaevalis, 11*, Turnhout, Buytaert, 1969; and the treatise *'De ordine palatii'* by the Archbishop of Rheims, Hincmar (845–82), in *Monumenta Germaniae Historica, 3*, Hannover, Gross-Schieffer, 1980.

16 For a general treatment of late medieval and Renaissance banking in Italy, see A. Grohmann, 'Credito ed economia urbana nel basso Medioevo', in *Atti del primo Convegno Nazionnale (4–6 giugno 1987) della Società Italiana degli storici dell'economia su 'Credito e sviluppo economico in Italia dal Medioevo all'Età Contemporanea'*, Verona, 1988, pp.23 ff.

17 While there was no central authority controlling the correctness of merchants' business dealings, the system in which banking activity was integrated in principle had a number of reference points that guaranteed the functioning of the financial market. The principal one was of course the primacy of Christianity and of the Church, depositary of tradition and doctrine, which laid down a set of theoretically inviolable principles for the granting of credit. The organisational structure of the papal administration and the rules governing questions of clergymen's property, together with the implicit assumption that the personal status of customers demanded that there be complete personal trust (and discretion) in relations with bankers, created the most reliable system of control on the activity of fifteenth-century merchant companies, namely market reputation.

18 For general references, see P. Prodi, 'La nascita dei Monti di Pietà: tra solidarismo cristiano e logica del profitto', *Annali dell'Istituto Italo-Germanico*, Trento, 1982, vol. VII. The fullest bibliography is in G. Todeschini, *Il prezzo della salvezza – Lessici medievali del pensiero economico*, Rome, Nuova Italia Scientifica, 1993.

19 There is an extensive literature on Franciscan thought and the debate pitting the Franciscans against the Dominicans over the *monti di pietà*. A general reference is O. Capitani (ed.), *Una economia politica nel Medioevo*, Bologna, Pàtron, 1987, particularly the chapters by G. Todeschini, 'Pietro di Giovanni Olivi come fonte per l'etica medievale' (pp.59–91), and A. Spicciani, 'Sant'Antonio, San Bernardino e Pier di Giovanni Olivi nel pensiero economico medievale' (pp.93–141).

20 Interest on loans to the needy is condemned not only for ethical reasons, but also on philosophical grounds as Aristotle clearly pointed out. Following Alexander of Hales and Albertus Magnus, St. Thomas condemned interest as contrary to commutative justice on a ground that proved a similitude to almost all his scholastic successors: interest is a price paid for the use of money; but, viewed from the standpoint of the individual holder, money is consumed in the act of being used; therefore, like wine, it has no use that can be separated from its substance as has, for example, a house; therefore charging for its use is charging for something that does not exist, which is illegitimate (usurious). This argument does not bear at all upon the question why interest is actually paid. But this question is the only one that is relevant to economic analysis.

21 This issue will be discussed below. With a view to covering the *monti's* operating expenses, the Fifth Lateran Council (1515–8), by explicit will of Pope Leo X (Giovanni de' Medici, reigned 1513–21), authorised the *monti* to demand 'reimbursement of expenses', in practice the payment of interest of up to 5 per cent per annum.

22 F. Melis, 'La grande conquista trecentesca del "credito di esercizio" e la tipologia dei suoi strumenti fino al XVI secolo', reprinted in A. Vannini Marx (ed.), *Credito, banche e investimenti (secolo XIII–XX)*, Florence, Le Monnier, 1985, p.25.

23 M. Fornasari, *Il Thesoro della città, op.cit.*, p.7.

24 The idea of the primacy of the Monte of Rome, implicit in the founding bull of Pope Paul III (1539), was made explicit in the bull published by Pius IV on 6 December

xxi

1561, which essentially affirmed that institution's power to transmit its privileges and indulgences to other *monti*. These two bulls are included in the preamble to the Statute of 1581. The same notion comes across in many other bulls issued in the sixteenth century concerning the Monte of Rome, collected in *Bolle e Privilegi del Sacro Monte della Pietà di Roma*, Rome, 1658, at ASMP.

I

THE HISTORICAL SETTING

Credit in the fourteenth to sixteenth centuries: the rules of the game

Credit and merchants in the fourteenth to sixteenth centuries

Between the fourteenth and sixteenth centuries credit activity was carried on simultaneously on different levels: at the top the major international banks, with far-flung business relations and large masses of capital, lending predominantly by means of bills of exchange and through networks of branches or affiliates in various financial centres; beneath these a host of loan and exchange banks specialising in small loans operating at the local level.[1] While banks that used financial expedients such as exchange or insurance contracts or sale and repurchase agreements in order to lend money ran no risk of falling foul of the strictures on usury, this was not the case of local banks, which openly carried on moneylending and charged explicit interest.[2] Moneylending could be lawfully practised on various grounds, notably under a grant of authorisation from a commune or principality. These licences had originally been issued to Christians and Jews alike, but with the passage of time most of them had fallen into the hands of Jews, who were subject to a different level of social acceptance for their practice and to different moral and religious rules.[3]

The papal administration's relative weight in the market enabled it to impose the 'rules of the game' from the twelfth century on, bending the interests of the merchants to a semblance of compliance with canon law and its ban on all apparently 'usurious' activity.[4] In reality, with the growth of commerce, the most widely held doctrine – based on a broad interpretation of certain passages of the Gospel and the Epistles of Saint Paul (excluding that lending at interest to a brother in need could be consistent with the principles of faith) and especially Thomas Aquinas and Aristotelian thought[5] – had extended the case of credit to the needy, which strictly speaking should not be credit at all but a gift

1

bestowed in the name of God,[6] to embrace the very different case of loans to risk-taking ventures.

Still, there existed various instruments that allowed a premium on credit to be lawfully obtained. The most common was the bill of exchange (*cambium per litteram*).[7] The bill did not involve usury, for where there was, strictly speaking, no loan or credit, there could be no usury, according to the dominant theory.[8] This made the banking profession socially acceptable, provided the banker operated on a large enough scale to conduct business in several financial centres[9] and thus to employ devices of this kind.[10] However, bills of exchange necessarily had to pass through a different company in the market abroad. That company could be a branch, an affiliate (or partnership with the 'major' partners of the holding company but with a local manager-partner, as was the case of great merchants like the Medici) or a correspondent. When the funds did not pass through other companies, so that, in the absence of capital movements, there was no exchange rate risk and the transaction constituted a loan in every respect except its form, the operation constituted so-called 'dry exchange' and was generally classed as a usurious loan.

At the apex of the profession were the great bankers, notably Italians, who dealt with the Roman Curia, boasted of being the pope's money-changers, held key positions in society, and were honoured and esteemed even though their guild, called simply *Arte del Cambio*, did not confer especially high social status.[11]

The interests affected by the *monti di pietà*

The above distinction should be borne in mind in assessing the impact of the birth of *monti di pietà* on the financial market of the period. In particular, it is useful to distinguish between the potential customers of the *monti* who dealt primarily with the great international merchants and those who instead dealt mainly with small local banks, and to consider the likely repercussions of the birth of the *monti* on the affairs of both the great merchant bankers and the petty moneylenders.

It was only on the fund-raising side that *monti* were in some degree potential rivals of the great merchant bankers, whose core customers were wealthy individuals in a position to be parties to transactions involving more than one financial centre, e.g. prelates at the papal court in Rome receiving remittances from their benefices. Quantification is difficult, but it is safe to say that the *monti* were able to tap only a portion of the funds that could be raised from aristocrats and clerics in the form of redeemable

The interests affected by the monti di pietà

annuities, outright deposits and bonds (*luoghi*).[12] The *monti* issued all these instruments in the course of their ordinary activity; indeed, they were spurred to do so by the continual need to raise funds for pledge loans. Favoured by privileges and indulgences, the *monti* soon became very competitive institutions in supplying fund-raising instruments. While non-interest-bearing deposits remained a marginal part of their activity, the forms of saving tied to bequests or endowments, generally consisting of perpetual, often redeemable annuities, were very popular, partly thanks to the Church's policy of favouring the *monti* with repeated indulgences and proclamations, the former designed to encourage the transfer of resources from the market to the *monti*, the latter not uncommonly a good deal more coercive (at the limit threatening excommunication of those whose wills did not provide for the *monte*'s share (*pars*)).[13] This was the only aspect of the activity of the *monti di pietà* that was likely to have a perceptible impact on the affairs of the great merchant bankers – perceptible, but not strong enough to cause them great concern.

On the lending side the great bankers had no reason to fear competition from the *monti*. Transactions large enough to justify using the complex exchange structures designed to shelter them from accusations of usury accounted for most of their business. Nor were their other credit operations, tied to merchandise trade or remittances of funds, threatened by the *monti*'s specialised activity of making small, short-term, secured and initially interest-free loans to local customers.

In summary, the *monti di pietà* posed a potential competitive threat chiefly to the (mostly Jewish) local moneylenders. The relationship between the two should therefore be examined from several angles, including but not limited to the religious question and the controversy between the Franciscans and the Dominicans. The overlap between their spheres of activity was significant despite the differences in their manner of conducting pledge-loan business with regard to the remuneration of capital (interest-free lending by the *monti* at the beginning), disposal of pledges in the event of default (with the *monti* paying over to the debtor any surplus on sale, and the local banks acting according to circumstances and usage) and auctions of expired pledges. We are, that is, dealing with a significant case of admittedly unequal economic competition at the dawn of modern banking. This is not to say that the *monti* invariably reduced the business of local banks or eliminated them altogether; for instance, in Bologna the local *monte* fulfilled a function complementary to that of the

Jewish bankers, so that its foundation coincided with a general expansion of the city's credit market.[14]

The licences under which local moneylenders operated often gave them a sort of 'competitive advantage' in a credit market segment where interest-bearing pledge loans prevailed.[15] It would be important to probe the difficult question of distinguishing between 'charitable' credit, the original task of the *monti di pietà*, and small loans for other purposes. Whether the interest rates on these loans were more or less governed by market forces or reflected the existence of vast positional rents (and were thus by implication truly usurious) is an issue that can be examined at length.

Avoidance of the rules on usury: do constraints stimulate innovation?

Rooting their speculation in the realities of their time, the theologians of the fourteenth to sixteenth centuries fashioned a moral philosophy that sought to influence and indeed to 'guide' human society, exerting an appreciable impact on the economy and the development of business and banking.[16] Not least among the consequences of the usury doctrine was that it stimulated the quest for licit means of earning a return on moneylending. These included, as noted, the bill of exchange, which disguised loan interest as speculative profits arising on exchange rate fluctuations.[17]

The Monte di Pietà of Rome itself used financial instruments that were not totally unlike bills of exchange. Early on, in taking deposits it issued *fedi di deposito* (deposit certificates) that came to be known as *cedole* (coupons). Whether these explicitly mentioned the interest rate is uncertain.[18] The first reference to *cedole* appears in the minutes of the directors' meeting of 10 July 1548.[19] The meeting decided to confirm Angelo Massimo in office as a *provvisore*, in view of the large number of *cedole* in circulation bearing his signature.[20] These *cedole* formally resembled the credit documents issued by merchant companies. The latter, however, were not signed when issued; rather, they were accepted when presented if the issuer's handwriting was recognised by his counter-party abroad, who checked the instrument presented to him against a retained copy.

The episode involving Angelo Massimo suggests that the Monte, like the large merchant companies, transacted business with counter-parties in faraway places.[21] But such activity does not appear to have represented a source of appreciable income for the Monte or a competitive threat to the great merchants. Among other considerations, the administration of the Monte was often headed by merchants and was structured vaguely along the lines of the apostolic administration, which made abundant use of merchant bankers for every kind of transaction.

There was thus only an apparent contrast between the doctrine on usury and the business activity that the leading bankers performed, especially in dealing with the Curia and the Church. Indeed, there is reason to believe that the ban on usury, far from braking the growth of credit and finance, was an important factor of innovation and change in banking practices. In the long term, however, this situation created a deep distortion in the operation of the banking and financial system in the countries tied most strongly to the Catholic tradition.

To be sure, re-reading history through the lens of a modern microeconomics textbook, we are led to say that the circumstances surrounding the birth of the *monti di pietà*, particularly with reference to the situation of local moneylenders, do not fit the concept of 'competition'. The picture does not accord with a static model of competition (the moneylenders probably sensed the aim of purely maximising profit, but such a concept was surely unknown to the founders of the *monti*), nor does it exemplify the Schumpeterian idea of dynamic competition, at once destructive and creative.[22]

The *monti di pietà*: between faith and the market

The *monti di pietà* phenomenon has therefore to be set in a complex context in which elements of both economic competition and political equilibria were at play. If the *monti* did not pose a competitive threat to great merchants, neither did they have anything to fear from the latter or the great banking houses, which dealt with a relatively limited number of wealthy customers unlikely to have much interest in 'consumer credit'. The causes of the decline of the great Italian banking houses lay elsewhere: from the end of the fifteenth century, with the *monti* still in their infancy, the Italians increasingly gave way on the international scene to rivals from northern Europe. The real competitive pressure of the *monti* concentrated on petty or local credit. The 'local shops' or 'banks not belonging to a guild'

> operated in the public money market through licences of varying degree of officialness that authorised as an exception what was called *exercitium fenoris*, i.e. lending at interest. This was a front line of banking, not infrequently difficult and uncomfortable –

performed in Italy by Tuscans and Lombards (names that generically embraced a diversity of provenance) and also by Jews – because the canon law on usury could easily strike this sector, regardless of the interest rates charged by these operators, who openly dealt in money without the camouflage of other transactions and could be defined as usurers pure and simple by Church doctrine.[23]

Jews did not completely control local credit, but they did dominate the market. Franco Pisa has found that, for several generations before the ghettos were established, local authorities had permitted Jews to lend money openly to commoners, including businessmen, using deposits and various forms of credit such as pledge loans, unsecured credit and advances on bills of exchange.[24] The Friars Minor adopted a very pragmatic line in combating 'usurers',[25] holding that even the interest rates charged by locally licensed moneylenders violated the dictates of doctrine and strongly criticising the fact that local authorities, without opposition and sometimes even with the assent of the Church, granted non-Christians official permission to carry on the money trade.[26]

But it would be wide of the mark to think that the paramount aim of those who founded the first *monti di pietà* was to seize control of local credit markets from the existing moneylenders. Such a view is accurate only in a few cases before the turn of the fifteenth century. More often, the birth of a *monte di pietà* proved generally beneficial for the local economy and expanded the overall size of the credit market. In a study of Jewish bankers in Bologna in the fifteenth century, M G Muzzarelli remarks that the Monte di Pietà of Bologna stands as

> an element of collaboration, both real and ideal, established with the Jews, as proof not only of the functionality of the Jewish presence but also of the ability of the city to shape constructive proposals pertaining to the economy and welfare.[27]

The overriding intention in setting up the *monti* was to assist the needy, independently of the market cost of money.[28] Later, the climate of rigour and zeal of the Counter-Reformation only radicalised the Franciscans' positions, so that excluding Jews from local credit markets became one of the avowed objectives of their campaign to establish *monti*. While the Franciscans and the Dominicans debated whether such an intervention in the credit market was licit, the new institutions continued to spread.[29]

The monti di pietà: between faith and the market

These motives and aims were certainly at work in Rome. Writing in favour of the Monte di Pietà of Rome, the anonymous author of a tract on 'the true state of the Jews in Rome' remarked that the Monte needed to be able 'to take the place of the lending that today is handled by Jews'.[30] In fact, the Monte did face competition from the Jewish moneylenders, who held auctions at which they sold off expired pledges without setting any limit on the right of the purchaser, unlike the Monte,[31] and were thus dangerous rivals on both fronts. Friction between administrators of *monti di pietà* and Jewish moneylenders over the rules on loans and auctions commonly arose in many cities.[32]

A degree of protectionism had also distinguished the Monte's policy in the past. In the meeting of 9 December 1570, the *deputati* discussed an announcement for the sale of pledges, with a warning to others not to organise similar events before or during the auction at the Monte.[33] The same meeting also approved permitting customers whose tickets had not expired to auction off the goods they had pledged.

However, on 17 October 1570 the *deputati* decided that if the purchaser of a pledge failed to pay the agreed price by the deadline (usually but not necessarily within fifteen days following the auction), the original pledger would be entitled to repurchase the goods upon payment not of the price agreed by the defaulting purchaser but of that determined by the appraiser; any downpayment received from the defaulting purchaser would be returned. This arrangement was apparently designed to improve the efficiency of sales, albeit not in a way that was particularly advantageous for the Monte. On 23 November 1571 it was decided after extensive discussion that any gains or surplus (*sopravanzo*) that the Jewish bankers realised on sales of pledges should be assigned to the Monte, in accordance with the indications of the apostolic administration.[34] On 5 July 1575 the directors returned to the matter and decided to submit a petition to the pope ('Our Lord') 'for a remedy, and to regulate the trade of the Jews'.[35] The meeting of 13 January 1579 resolved to request the cardinal camerlengo to assign a judge in disputes with the Jews, without prejudice to the jurisdiction of the judge of the Monte. In the meeting of 11 March 1581 the directors approved a draft agreement to be proposed to representatives of the Jewish bankers for the commencement of auditing of the accounts on gains from the disposal of pledges. Under the terms of this agreement the Jewish bankers undertook to return all gains realised and withheld from 5 April 1570 onwards that they were unable to prove with a receipt, third-party testimony or public admission of the parties, confirmed by the account books, that they had returned the amounts in question to the borrowers. However, the accord allowed them to calculate the amount to be returned net of any losses on disposals of pledges belonging to the same counter-party. On 12 December 1581 it was ordered that a minute of the nineteen decrees bearing on the question be drawn up.[36]

Relations with the Jews long remained an open question for the administration of the Monte di Pietà and were on occasion the focus of its meetings. On 14 May 1565, for example, the administration dealt again with the types of deposit the Monte could accept, the competition of Jewish pawnbrokers in auctions and the question of whether or not the pawnbrokers should be allowed to deposit the pledged goods in their possession with the Monte.[37] Financial relations again came under discussion on 15 February 1568, when it was decided to prohibit the Monte's cashier from issuing *cedole* ('his receipts') for deposits made by Jews in connection with financial transactions deemed to be in violation of the rules.[38] On 2 May 1584 the directors decided to appeal to the pope to allow at least one representative of the Monte to attend the Jewish-run auctions as an observer and to establish a permanent auction site.[39] The request appears to have been promptly accepted, for the directors' meeting of 8 June 1584 determined that the Monte's two observers at Jewish auctions could not put in bids for their own or others' account or participate in any other way.

By the end of the sixteenth century the Monte was the dominant force in the local credit market in Rome, holding virtually absolute sway in the field of small loans for presumably welfare-related purposes. During the sixteenth and seventeenth centuries several popes, without abolishing the ghetto, restored some freedom of action to the Jewish moneylenders in Rome and the other papal cities where Jews were allowed to live.[40] Among them was Sixtus V, remembered as a competent administrator of the papal finances.[41] With ups and downs in their freedom of action and their stock of capital, the Jewish moneylenders remained active in Rome until the papal licences were definitively revoked in 1682.[42]

Rome in the sixteenth century: an economic and political centre

Between the fourteenth and sixteenth centuries Rome presented a dual economic reality.[43] While the city owed its importance as a business centre chiefly to its links with the temporal interests of the Church and the presence of the papal court,[44] it was also the seat of a lively local economy that had attained considerable size by the second half of the sixteenth century. The economic activities revolving about the papal court and the Apostolic Chamber ensured that Rome was one of the principal financial centres of Europe up to the end of the fifteenth century, and, although its importance diminished, the city remained prominent in international finance even after the centre of gravity of European trade had shifted from the Mediterranean to the Atlantic and following the Protestant Reformation.

When the pope resided in Rome, there was an enormous market for every manner of article to satisfy the needs of the prelates, pilgrims, notables and merchants who flocked around the Curia and the pope, and an abundant flow of remittances and offerings from practically every corner of Europe and the known world.[45] The Roman Curia's spiritual and temporal relations with all the known world necessitated the creation of a highly ramified network of correspondents charged with collecting and remitting offerings and revenues. Until the Reformation cast doubt on the primacy of the Church in northern and central Europe, the scale of these flows was such that the banking and merchant companies active in Rome could concentrate most of their operations in the field of finance, advancing credit to customers, handling the remittance of funds to the holders of benefices or to the Apostolic Chamber, and taking substantial deposits from the court prelates, almost invariably members of the great families of Europe. The importance of the flows of funds from benefices and prebends, reflected in the surviving account books of the companies operating in Rome, is evidenced above all by the pivotal position of this issue alongside theological questions in Luther's dispute with Rome.

Credit and business in the shadow of the papal court

A banker dealing directly with the Curia had a chance to exploit that connection in order to pursue the even more lucrative prospect of becoming private banker to many prelates.[46] Most banking houses were also merchant firms and could therefore supply not only financial services but also items that had to be imported from afar. Although they sometimes handled shipments of grain or other commodities, most of their trade involved goods destined for wealthy customers. Thus Rome offered major opportunities to the merchant bankers and was a traditionally 'liquid' market, with an abundance of capital available for credit and for the financing of purchases and business transactions.

In the sixteenth century, however, the Protestant Reformation and the gradual migration of world trade from the Mediterranean to the north of Europe eroded Rome's position as a financial centre. In commercial dealings, moreover, the Italians steadily gave up ground first to the German bankers (the Fuggers and Welsers, most notably) and then to the English and Dutch. Towards the end of the century this decline was temporarily reversed with the revival of Genoa and Piacenza.[47]

Although the period of their greatest splendour had passed and their political role was greatly reduced, the Italian states continued to be important players in the international economy. The founding of the Monte di Pietà of Rome in 1539 fell in a relatively dynamic economic context, but one marked by striking inequalities and still scarred by memories of the sack of the city in 1527. The effects of the good times and bad of the great merchants were somewhat muted for the city as a whole. Indeed, the poor, the small artisans and even some of the merchants and what we are tempted to call an *ante litteram* bourgeoisie formed an economic fabric that had limited relations with the court, a 'city within the city', and reaped relatively few benefits from the business dealings that revolved around it and the papal administration. It was this segment of the Roman market and its needs for business and consumption finance, traditionally the preserve of local moneylenders and loan and exchange banks, that the Monte was intended to serve.

The local economy

The local economy's role had emerged more clearly during the Great Schism and the frequent absences of the pope from Rome in the fifteenth century. By the end of the sixteenth century it consisted of a solid fabric of artisanal enterprise, shops and small merchant ventures.[48] A description by Amintore Fanfani of the situation of local craft production a few decades later, during the 'crisis of the seventeenth century', gives an idea of its importance:

> Traditional forms coexisted with innovations in the organisation and regulation of work. In the artisans' shops masters continued to work with a few partners and assistants. In 1622 there were 6,609 shop owners and 17,504 apprentices in Rome, so that an average of 1.18 owners and 3.14 apprentices worked in each of the city's 5,578 shops'.[49]

The figures for the turn of the century were probably not far different from these, which refer to conditions after prolonged recession. Consequently, the more than 20,000 persons employed in the shops made up a very sizeable share of the city's population, variously estimated at between 50,000 and 70,000 at the end of the sixteenth century.

The papal administration

The city also owed its importance as a business centre to the particular structure of the papacy's financial administration. The linchpin of the administration of the pope's temporalities was the Apostolic Chamber, endowed with broad and varied powers and entrusted with two pre-eminent tasks – the government of the papal states and the management of the pope's finances resulting from his position as both temporal and spiritual ruler. It was headed by the Chamberlain, a bishop.[50] Under the Chamberlain came the Apostolic Treasurer, a bishop or other high prelate, who directly supervised payments, collections and audits, and dealt with the bankers from the fifteenth century onwards, when it was no longer the practice for the Treasurer to keep the papal monies in a chest in his own custody. From the early fifteenth century, in fact, the treasury's funds were deposited with one of the banking companies that dealt with the Curia, whose director assumed the title of *depositarius*. The papal account was in the name of the depositary, who entered all the in-payments received and out-payments made on behalf of his principal. The Apostolic Chamber kept an authenticated copy of the book in which the depositary entered all receipts and disbursements in chronological order, with an analytical index of the transactions. The original book was kept in Italian. Two authenticated copies translated into Latin, one for the depositary himself, were made by a notary. These books, called *Introitus et Exitus*, summarised the pope's financial accounts and were audited and approved each month by an official appointed by the Chamberlain.

The Monte's evolving role

The early years

A number of events stand out as landmarks in the history of the Monte from its birth in 1539 to its radical transformation with the conferral of the Bank of Deposits for Judicial Proceedings of the papal state in 1584. These include the incorporation of the Ospedale dei Boemi in 1546, the merger with the Company of

Table 1 *Estimated operating expenses of the Monte di Pietà of Rome, 1540–50* [52]

Year	Certain	Estimated	Total
1540	sc. 22 b. 87½	sc. 202 b. 30	sc. 225 b. 17½
1541	sc. 89 b. 37½	sc. 208 b. 95	sc. 298 b. 32½
1542	sc. 136 b. 87½	sc. 213 b. 70	sc. 350 b. 57½
1543	sc. 175 b. 75	sc. 217 b. 60	sc. 393 b. 35
1544	sc. 200 b. 75	sc. 220	sc. 420 b. 75
1545	sc. 201 b. 75	sc. 220	sc. 421 b. 75
1546	*sc. 201 b. 75*	sc. 220	sc. 421 b. 75
1547	*sc. 201 b. 75*	sc. 220	sc. 421 b. 75
1548	*sc. 201 b. 75*	sc. 220	sc. 421 b. 75
1549	*sc. 201 b. 75*	sc. 220	sc. 421 b. 75
1550	*sc. 201 b. 75*	sc. 220	sc. 421 b. 75
Total	**sc. 1836 b. 12½**	**sc. 2382 b. 55**	**sc. 4218 b. 67½**

Note: *italics* = estimated data, **bold** = sourced data (applies to all tables)

San Bernardo in 1551, the preparation of the first draft statutes in 1557, the Borromean statutes of 1565, and the publication of the first official text of the statutes and internal regulations in 1581.

The Rome Monte was established the same year as its counterpart in Naples.[51] This coincidence probably reflects joint action on the part of Spanish and papal diplomacy, a supposition partly based on the role played in the creation of the Monte by the then protector of the Order of Saint Francis, Cardinal Quinones, who as confessor of Emperor Charles V was surely the Roman prelate closest to the Spanish crown. The period up to 1584 was perhaps that in which the reality of the Monte corresponded most closely to the purposes and principles for which it was established. The members of the congregation were directly involved in the Monte's affairs and most of its funding came from private contributions together with several extraordinary operations, i.e. mergers or attempted mergers with hospitals and other charitable institutions. These years were marked by a chronic shortage of funds, operational difficulties and slow progress towards the definition of a clear hierarchical and organisational structure, which was only accomplished with the statutes of 1581.

Although we have no source document summarising the Monte's operating costs in its first years of activity, annual expenses and cash requirements can be estimated with reasonable approximation on the basis of general references to the Monte's ordinary activity, wage bill and rent payments. It is more arduous to make assumptions regarding the sources of the funds that were used to cover current outlays. The relevant data are lacking, although we do know that the shortfall of reliable funding prompted the congregation to call on the members of the Company to subscribe more capital. A watershed was the assignment of the Bank of Deposits to the Monte in 1584 with a brief issued by Pope Gregory XIII, marking the transformation of the charitable establishment into a sort of state agency with pre-eminent tasks within the papal administration.[53] Following this change, the Monte, no longer chronically short of funds, was able to reduce its reimbursement of expenses on loans and phase it out altogether for amounts of less than 30 *scudi*.[54] The events of 1584 brought the Monte's early years to a close.

The significance of the change is nicely summarised by C M Travaglini:

> It should be recalled that the Monte di Pietà took several decades to establish itself and gradually to extend its functions from those of a charitable institution with a modest activity of lending to become the most important financial institution operating in Rome. The opening of a Deposit Bank alongside and under the control of the Loan Bank made a decisive contribution to the Monte's growth. Great impetus was imparted to this felicitous idea from 1584 onwards, following Gregory XIII's decision[55] that all legal deposits exceeding 5 *scudi* had to be made exclusively with the Monte's Deposit Bank. This created a virtuous circle, reinforced not only by the size of the legal deposits but also by the image of soundness that the institution projected. The funds deposited did not remain idle in the Monte's strongboxes. Some of them were put back into circulation through a progressive extension of pledge lending in response to strong demand, which in turn was stimulated in the course of time by a gradual reduction in interest rates and eventually the ntroduction in 1636 of interest-free credit for transactions of not more than 30 *scudi* each.[56]

The turning point and after

The Monte actually changed face after 1584, assuming a role in the public administration for the first time and becoming a public entity in virtually every respect. This shift was confirmed by the gradual change in the sources of funding. The decline in the role of private providers of funds was reflected by the reversion to interest-free lending.[57] As the importance of private capital declined, debt securities (*cedole* and *luoghi*) became increasingly pivotal, reflecting the Monte's 'impact' on the local economy and the public's accurate perception that the Monte's debt issues were equivalent to state debt.

Nonetheless, more than a century still had to pass before the integration of the Monte into the papal administration would be complete. This was achieved in 1743, when the Monte was appointed to manage the papal treasury as depositary of the Apostolic Chamber,[58] a position until then always held by private bankers. The last great change for the Monte before the fall of the papal state came with its appointment to run the state mint during the nineteenth century. Following the Risorgimento and the unification of Italy, when the functions that had been centralised in the Monte were divided among different institutions, the Monte sought to return to its original vocation of charity and welfare.

The history of the Monte di Pietà of Rome as an independent entity ended with its merger into Cassa di Risparmio di Roma in 1937. The latter took over the Monte's pawnbroking operation and ran it until the successive mergers of the Cassa with Banco di Santo Spirito and of the latter with Banco di Roma gave birth to Banca di Roma. The new bank succeeded to the Monte's activity, which it continues to perform in the Monte's historic building at No. 33 Piazza del Monte di Pietà in Rome.

Notes

1   For general reference, see C.M. Cipolla, 'Il governo della moneta a Firenze e a Milano nei secoli XIV–XVI', in *La repubblica internazionale del denaro*, edited by A. De Maddalena and H. Kellenbenz, Bologna, Il Mulino, 1986.

2   See O. Capitani (ed.), *Una economia politica nel Medioevo, op. cit.*, particularly the previously cited chapters by G. Todeschini and A. Spicciani and that by J. Kirshner and K. Lo Prete, 'I trattati di Pietro di Giovanni Olivi sui contratti di vendita, di usura e di restituzione: economia dei minori francescani o opere minori?', pp.143–91. See also R. de Roover, *Money, Banking, and Credit in Mediaeval Bruges: Italian Merchant-Bankers, Lombards, and Money-Changers*, Cambridge, Mass., The Mediaeval Academy of America, 1948; idem, *The Rise and Decline of the Medici Bank, 1397–1494*, Cambridge, Mass., Harvard University Press, 1963; reprinted New York, Norton, 1966, pp.14–20; F. Melis, 'Industria, Commercio, Credito', in *Un'altra Firenze*, Florence, 1971; idem, *Documenti per la storia economica dei secoli XIII–XVI*, Florence, Leo S. Olschki, 1972, pp.88 ff.

3   Various sources can be cited on the acceptability of a Jewish banker's charging explicit interest on loans. A number of less than banal questions posed by Jewish thinkers and rabbis as well as Christians concerned lending to co-religionists (this too at no interest?), the extensibility of municipal licences to cover such cases, the 'moral' acceptability of moneylending licences, the definition of usury, the line to take with the Christian authorities. The literature on these issues is abundant. Here I shall only recall G. Todeschini, 'Gli ebrei medioevali come minoranza attiva nella storiografia italiana degli ultimi trent'anni', in *La storia degli ebrei nell'Italia medioevale: tra filologia e metodologia*, Bologna, Istituto per i beni artistici e culturali della regione Emilia-Romagna, 1990; A. Tenenti, 'Un primo bilancio', in *Gli ebrei e Venezia (secoli*

Notes to Chapter I

XIV–XVIII), Proceedings of the international conference organised by the Istituto di storia della società e dello stato veneziano della Fondazione Giorgio Cini, Venice, 5–10 June 1983, edited by G. Cozzi and R. Bonfil, Milan, 1987; S. Simonsohn, 'Lo stato attuale della ricerca storica sugli ebrei in Italia', in *Italia Judaica I*, Proceedings of the first international conference held in Bari on 18–22 May 1981, Rome, 1983.

4   A diversity of factors moulded the credit market; it would be reductive to state that the authority of the Church enabled it to regulate economic custom rigorously. The market's formal acceptance of certain restrictions and moral principles reflected the fact that the merchants found such a setting worked to their advantage. Max Weber addresses this point in *The Protestant Ethic and the Spirit of Capitalism*. On the doctrinal aspects of the debate, see Origine, *In Matthaeum (versio latina antiqua)*, Berlin, Klostermann-Benz, 1935 and subsequent years), and Pietro di Tarantasia, 'Quodlibet', *Revue de Théologie ancienne et médiévale*, Paris, Glorieux, 1937, vol. 9, pp.242–75. The original manuscript of Pietro di Giovanni Olivi, *Super Matthaeum*, is in the Biblioteca Antoniana of Padua, ms 336.

5   Saint Bernardine of Siena, *Quadragesimale de Christiana Religione*, Opera II, Florence, Quaracchi, 1950; Thomas Aquinas, *Summa Theologiae*; Alexander of Hales, *Summa Theologica*; Abelard, *op. cit.* For reference, see M.F. Barry, *The Vocabulary of the Moral-Ascetical Works of Saint Ambrose. A Study in Latin Lexicography*, Washington, The Catholic University of America, 1926, Patristic Studies, 10. Aristotle, *Politics* (I–II), in *Aritoteles Latinus* XXVII, Paris, Michaud-Quantin, 1961.

6   Luke 6:35.

7   A bill of exchange involved the transaction of bills payable in a distant place and often in a different currency, with interest concealed in the price of the bill. This was perfectly licit, as the transaction did not involve a loan but a sale or exchange of foreign currency. The classic structure involved four parties, two in the domestic market (the 'deliverer', or buyer of the bill and hence of foreign currency, and the 'taker', or issuer of the bill) and two abroad (the 'payer' and 'payee'). The final recipient of the funds actually corresponds to a borrower receiving cash for a bill payable in another place. This generates a subsequent flow of currencies, exchanged at different rates than the original ones. The second-leg exchange rates could easily incorporate interest, but this would take the form of profit on exchange. In the account books of fifteenth- and sixteenth-century bankers, discount operations rarely appear whereas exchange transactions are numerous. There was usually no interest account, not even in the 'secret account books', for such a practice would have been risky. Instead, there was an account called 'exchange profits and losses', which was taken into 'bank surpluses and deficits', corresponding to the profit and loss account. See F. Melis, *Documenti per la storia economica dei secoli XIII–XVI*, *op. cit.*, pp.88–103.

8   Saint Bernardine, in *Quadragesimale de Evangelio Aeterno*, Sermon 36, Art. 36, Ch. 1 and Art. 2, Ch. 1, said that *'usura solum in mutuo cadit'*.

9   Foreign exchange transactions in places other than that where the contract was made (through 'bills of exchange') were the most common method of moneylending that skirted the accusation of usury, with the interest charged by the merchant banker cloaked in profit from forward exchange rate risk. The foreign currency market could be very volatile, so that a Florence–London–Florence exchange order, for example, that formally required two months' value-dating could carry considerable capital risk. In the absence of hedging, this risk was full. The banker and the customer stood the same chance of making a capital gain or loss. If a currency's exchange rate with another fluctuated by 3–4 per cent in a month, which was not exceptional, the merchant could find himself making an interest-free loan (or even one bearing negative interest) or the customer having to pay interest of 30–40 per cent per annum. Whereas a formal loan contract at 5 per cent interest would have been considered usury, an exchange transaction that was very onerous because of exchange rate fluctuations was completely licit. De Roover, in *The Rise and Decline of the Medici Bank*, *op.cit.*, Chapter VI, maintains that the interest rates charged by the principal merchant companies in the European market, always concealed in complex exchange transactions, averaged between 12 and 4 per cent in the fourteenth century. In sixteenth-century Rome, the interest rate on public debt securities ranged between approximately 7 and 12 per cent (see F. Colzi, 'I Monti del popolo romano', doctoral dissertation, VIII ciclo, Università degli Studi di Bari, Table III.a, p.146). Bearing in mind that sovereign debt is usually at a premium with respect to private debt, the interest rates charged to reputable debtors in Rome

during the same period were probably not unlike those de Roover considers the reference rates for the 1400s. Although this involves considerable conjecture, particularly as regards the level of interest rates in the first half of the sixteenth century, it raises the question of whether the inflationary impact of the influx of American silver had still to be felt in Rome in the second half of the sixteenth century.

10   De Roover remarks: 'What was dry exchange. It was a product of the usury doctrine; therefore it is without analogy in modern business. It can best be described as a transaction involving *cambium et recambium*, or exchange and rechange, but without any final settlement taking place. In fact, it mattered little whether or not the contracting parties took the trouble of actually making out and dispatching bills of exchange' (*The Rise and Decline of the Medici Bank, op.cit.*, p.132). Since theologians prohibited this as a practice *in fraudem usurarum*, to carry on credit activity it was essential for merchants to be able to act effectively on their correspondents or affiliates for the issue of letters of credit. This was no doubt a spur to the internationalisation of the merchant companies.

11   Small moneylenders, who generally could not resort to devices or contrivances such as exchange contracts, were often branded as usurers regardless of the interest rate they charged or the licences they had received. The consequences of this accusation were very grave; usurers lived under the ban of the Church and society, were deprived of Christian burial and were even debarred from making valid wills. See de Roover, *The Rise and Decline of the Medici Bank, op. cit.*, pp.14 ff.

12   The 'yield' on securities issued by the Monte di Pietà of Rome was not intended as interest although it resembled interest in every respect. The 'premium' was justified by the rents or benefits of the underlying guarantees, as in the case of other Roman debt funds. Pursuant to the decretal instituting the first debt fund in papal history, the Monte della Fede, authorised by Clement VII in 1526, these had to be secured at least by a building. Holders of shares of the debt therefore did not receive 'interest' but 'rent'. The securities issued by the Monte di Pietà were backed mainly by real property. See Colzi, *op. cit.*, pp.2–3.

13   Various resolutions use the word *pars* to designate the share of the bequests and legacies that notaries had to remember to have the testator mention; see ASMP, '*Registri dei Decreti di Congregazione 1540–1566*', Tome 39, pp.V–XI. The idea of trying to persuade the pope to make this act mandatory was considered on several occasions, especially during the Rome Monte's difficult first years, but there is no record of the enactment of such a measure.

14   M. Fornasari, *Il Thesoro della città, op. cit.*, pp.155 ff.

15   Local moneylenders also engaged in riskier types of lending. Consider, further, that small loans were not limited to consumer credit (and this in turn did not necessarily coincide with 'lending to those in need', where charging interest was a grave offence), but included business loans to artisans and shopkeepers.

16   This section is based partly on F. Arcelli, 'Quando i vincoli creano l'innovazione: un parallelo storico', *Confronto*, 1 (January–June 1997), pp.39–44.

17   In reality, the doctrine on usury left room for business transactions whose effect was the same as that of contracts that were considered illicit, thus creating an impediment more formal than substantial to the development of the banking enterprise. For the upright Christian, what counted was not the substance of the question but whether the appearance of his business was legitimate or illicit. Francesco di Marco Datini of Prato, whom de Roover calls 'ruthless and grasping', could boast in writing that he had never made illicit profits (de Roover, *The Rise and Decline of the Medici Bank, op. cit.*, p.12). There is a long history of 'conferences' between theologians and bankers on the problem of the licit operation of banks. Two well-known examples are those held in Antwerp in 1517 and 1532, discussed at length by Jan A. Goris, *Etudes sur les colonies marchandes méridionales a Anvers de 1488 à 1567*, Louvain, 1925, pp.507–45. On the bill of exchange, see de Roover, *ibid.*, pp.10–20.

18   See C.M. Travaglini, 'Le Origini del Banco dei Depositi del Monte di Pietà di Roma e le prime emissioni di cedole (secc. XVI–XVII)', *Atti del Secondo Convegno Nazionale della Società Italiana degli Storici dell'Economia (4–6 marzo 1993)*, Bologna, Monduzzi, 1996, pp.477–82.

19   ASMP, '*Registri dei Decreti di Congregazione 1540–1566*', Tome 39, p.XI, c.22.

20   Angelo Massimo died in 1550, before the meeting of 18 May 1550; ASMP, '*Registri dei Decreti di Congregazione 1540–1566*', Tome 39, p.XV, c.29. The official reason for his reinstatement in office in 1548 is interesting, namely that the replacement of a director

Notes to Chapter I

who had signed a large part of the deposit certificates issued by the Monte might be prejudicial for the holders of those certificates.

21 Otherwise, replacing the official who materially drew up the *cedole* would not have been a matter of concern; a few days would have sufficed to inform correspondents. It is also possible that the approach of the Jubilee of 1550 prompted the institution to initiate correspondence activity for the remittance of funds to Rome on behalf of pilgrims, and may even have led to the request for a special privilege, but this is pure speculation.

22 J.A. Schumpeter, *The Theory of Economic Development. An Inquiry into Profits, Capital, Credit, Interest and the Business Cycle*, New York, Oxford University Press, 1961, pp.212–55.

23 F. Pisa, 'Attività bancarie locali nell'Italia dei secoli XIV–XVI', *Zakhor – rivista di storia degli ebrei d'Italia – Mercanti e banchieri ebrei*, 1997, no. 1, pp.114–15.

24 F. Pisa, *op. cit.*, pp.113–49.

25 'Usury' did not denote exorbitant interest but any interest charged, regardless of whatsoever economic or market-related consideration.

26 For general reference, see O. Capitani (ed.), *Una economia politica nel Medioevo, op. cit.*; O. Capitani (ed.), *L'etica economica medievale*, Bologna, Il Mulino, 1974; J. Mossay (ed.), *Thesaurus Sancti Gregorii Nazianzeni (Orationes, Epistolae, Testamentum*, Louvain-la-Neuve, Cetedoc, 1990; S. Bonaventura da Bagnoregio, *Opera Omnia*, Florence, Quaracchi, 1882 and subsequent years; J. Hamesse (ed.), *Thesaurus Librorum Sententiarum Petrii Lombardi*, Louvain-la-Neuve, Cetedoc, 1991.

27 M.G. Muzzarelli, *Banchi ebraici a Bologna nel XV secolo*, Bologna, Il Mulino, 1994, pp.21–2.

28 The definition of 'need' was not a self-evident economic concept, however. That indeterminacy may help to account for the adoption of such a radical and generalist approach to the questions of credit. See R.M. Kidd, 'Wealth and beneficence in the Pastor. Epistles: An Inquiry into a 'Bourgeois' Form of Early Christianity', Dissertation at Duke University, Durham, NC, 1990.

29 For a general treatment of the debate between the Franciscans and the Dominicans, see L. Vereeke, *Da Guglielmo di Ockham a Sant'Alfonso de' Liguori. Saggi di storia della teologia morale moderna (1300–1787)*, Milan, Edizioni Paoline, 1990, chapters III–VIII. The debate, centring on the 'reimbursement of expenses' or 'just interest' of 5 per cent that the *monti* were authorised to demand following the Fifth Lateran Council, dragged on for years. The issue is also addressed by B. Nelson, *Usura e Cristianesimo. Per una storia della genesi dell'etica moderna*, Florence, Sansoni, 1967, pp.25–45. See also R. de Roover, 'The Concept of the Just Price', *Journal of Economic History*, 1958, vol. 18, pp.539–66, which focuses on the merchant companies. Also, O. Capitani (ed.), *Una economia politica nel Medioevo, op. cit.*, particularly the chapters by G. Todeschini, A. Spicciani, and J. Kirshner and K. Lo Prete.

30 Anonymous, *Il vero stato degli Ebrei in Roma*, Rome, Stamperia del Varese, 1668, cited by Tosi, *op. cit.*, p.79, and Tamilia, *op. cit.*, p.12, who considers it a useful source on the history of the Monte.

31 Tosi, *op. cit.*, Ch. V, describes at length the role of Jewish moneylenders in the Roman credit market. Being non-competitive in auction activity constituted a major handicap for the Monte during its start-up.

32 See the cases mentioned by A. Antoniazzi Villa, *Un processo contro gli ebrei nella Milano del 1488. Crescita e declino della comunità ebraica lombarda alla fine del Medioevo*, Bologna, Il Mulino, 1986.

33 For this and the immediately following citiations from the directors' resolutions, see ASMP, '*Nota Decretorum Congregationis 1540–1604*', references to the years 1570–81.

34 The question of these surpluses, or differences between the amount realised at auction and that actually owed by the debtor, posed ethical difficulties for the Jewish bankers as well. The practice of withholding *sopravanzi* was sufficiently widespread for an entire article of the Statutes of 1581 (capitolo XXVI) to be dedicated to regulating the assignment of such gains to the Monte.

35 ASMP, '*Nota Decretorum Congregationis 1540–1604*', reference to 1575.

36 ASMP, '*Nota Decretorum Congregationis 1540–1604*', references to 1581. The summary record was drawn up 'by act of Bernardino Pascatio, capitular notary'.

37 ASMP. '*Nota Decretorum Congregationis 1540–1604*', references to 1565.

38 ASMP, 'Nota Decretorum Congregationis 1540–1604', references to 1568. This is indirect evidence that the rules had probably not yet brought the hoped-for benefits to the indigent. In addition, by discouraging buyers or at least depressing prices, they must have been an impediment to the ready liquidation of goods held by the Monte.

39 For this and the subsequent resolution, ASMP, 'Nota Decretorum Congregationis 1540–1604', references to 1584.

40 On relations between the papacy and the Jews, see S. Simonsohn, *The Apostolic See and the Jews (1492–1555). Documents and History*, Toronto, 1988–91, L. Poliakov, *Les banquiers Juifs e le Saint-Siège du XIII au XVII siècle*, Paris, 1967, and P. Prodi, *Il Sovrano Pontefice. Un corpo e due anime: la monarchia papale nella prima età moderna*, Bologna, Il Mulino, 1982.

41 Sixtus V (1585–90) was expert at devising new sources of finance for his countless works in progress and outstanding commitments. His reign saw the famous 'sale of major public offices' and extensive recourse to public debt in the form of *luoghi*. See Tosi, *op.cit.*, pp.147–9; F. Colzi, *op. cit.*, pp.128 ff.; F. Piola Caselli, 'Aspetti del debito pubblico nello Stato Pontificio: gli uffici vacabili', *Annali della facoltà di scienze politiche dell'Università degli studi di Perugia (1970–1972)*, 1972; and L. Falchi, 'Sisto V e l'Annona: l'eredità di un secolo', *Dimensioni e problemi della ricerca storica*, 1990, no. 2, pp.91–108.

42 An edict issued by Innocent XI (1676–89) on 30 October 1682 banned all lending at interest by Jews.

43 For general reference, see L. von Pastor, *History of the Popes from the Close of the Middle Ages* (Italian translation: *Storia dei Papi dalla fine del Medio Evo compilata col sussidio dell'Archivio Segreto Pontificio e di molti altri Archivi*, Rome, 1950–65), Torino, Einaudi; J. Delumeau, *Vie économique et sociale de Rome dans la seconde moitié du XVI siècle*, Paris, Boccard, 1957–9, two vols.), pp.665–88, particularly on monetary questions; and F. Gregorovius's landmark *History of the City of Rome in the Middle Ages* (Italian translation: *Storia della città di Roma nel Medioevo*, Rome, 1901).

44 R. de Roover, *The Rise and Decline of the Medici Bank*, *op. cit.*, and M. Cassandro, *Il libro giallo di Ginevra della compagnia fiorentina di Antonio della Casa e Simone Guadagni, 1453–1454*, Prato, Istituto Internazionale di Storia Economica F. Datini, 1976, pp.29–30. Naturally, whenever the pope left Rome the capital flows, individuals and interests attached to the court, including the merchant banking companies, followed his movements.

45 The scale of the papal treasury's dealings is conveyed by the fact that Scandinavia, Iceland and even Greenland paid tribute to Rome. Tribute was generally paid in kind, the goods were then sold locally or in northern European markets and the proceeds were transferred to Rome. In 1492 the bishop of Greenland won an exemption on the grounds that his diocese was too poor to pay tribute. See Henry S. Lucas, *Medieval Economic Relations between Flanders and Greenland*, 1937, vol. 12, pp.167–81.

46 Prelates at court visited the benefices they held only rarely and generally entrusted bankers with remitting their revenues. In addition, although the rule that the Church inherited the worldly possessions of deceased priests was mainly honoured in the breach, it compelled priests wishing to safeguard their heirs to have solid relationships with their bankers. The latter were not subject to any special controls and were bound to maintain the utmost confidentiality on the deposits in their care, a rule of conduct not unlike that mandated by banking secrecy today. See J. Favier, *Les finances pontificales a l'époque du Grand Schisme d'Occident (1378–1409)*, Paris, Boccard – Bibliothéque des écoles françaises d'Athènes et de Rome, no. 211, pp.72 ff.

47 F. Braudel, *La dinamica del capitalismo*, Bologna, Il Mulino, 1977, pp.43 ff. describes the role of Genoese merchants and bankers and of the fairs of Piacenza in the trade of precious metals from the Americas. From 1620–1 onwards Piacenza faded as a commercial centre and Amsterdam rose to unchallenged primacy.

48 The end of the Babylonian captivity stimulated Italian manufacturing and offered new prospects to Roman merchants, artisans and bankers. L. Palermo underscores two important developments during the papacy of Boniface IX (1389–1404), namely the institutional reform of 1398, by which the commune of Rome was dissolved and the pope took municipal affairs into his own hands, and the reorganisation of the financial administration of the papacy and the Apostolic Chamber, which imparted impetus to the growth of the Roman financial and commercial market. See L. Palermo, 'L'anno santo dei mercanti: dibattito storiografico e documenti economici sul cosiddetto giubileo del 1400', in *Studi in onore di Paolo Brezzi*, Rome, 1988. See also A. Esch, 'La

Notes to Chapter I

fine del libero comune di Roma nel giudizio dei mercanti fiorentini. Lettere romane degli anni 1395–1398 nell'Archivio Datini', *Bollettino dell'Istituto Storico Italiano per il Medio Evo*, 1976–7, pp.235–77. For an overview of the Roman situation at the end of the fifteenth century and information on foreign, especially Tuscan, investments in Rome, see A. Ait, 'Credito e iniziativa commerciale: aspetti dell'attività economica a Roma nella seconda metà del XV secolo', *Atti del primo Convegno Nazionale (4–6 giugno 1987) della Società Italiana degli storici dell'economia su 'Credito e sviluppo economico in Italia dal Medio Evo all'Età Contemporanea'*, Verona, 1988, pp.67 ff.

49 A. Fanfani, *Storia Economica. Parte I, Antichità – Medioevo – Età Moderna*, Turin, UTET, 1968, pp.565–6.

50 This summary description of the papal administration draws on F. Arcelli, 'A Banking Enterprise at the Papal Court: the Company of Antonio Della Casa and Jacopo di Michele di Corso Donati (1438–1440)', *The Journal of European Economic History*, no. 1 (Spring 1996), vol. 25, pp.9–32, and *idem*, 'La costituzione della compagnia di Antonio della Casa e Jacopo di Michele di Corso Donati presso la corte pontificia (1438–1440)', *Studi Romani*, vol. XLV, no. 1–2 (January–June 1997), pp.5–26. A brief description of the operation of the papal administration and the changes in its organisation in the fifteenth centuries is found in R. de Roover, *The Rise and Decline of the Medici Bank, op.cit.*, pp.196–200. The Chamberlain (*Camerlengo*) who presided the Apostolic Chamber should not be confused with the cardinal camerlengo, who performed his duties within the College of Cardinals and represented the political authority of the state during vacancies of the Holy See. Rarely did the two coincide. See the excellent study by J. Favier, *Le finances pontificales, op. cit.*, pp.72–92.

51 For general discussion and bibliography, see L. De Rosa, *Banchi pubblici, banchi privati e monti di pietà a Napoli nei secoli XVI e XVIII, op. cit.*

52 Sources: Tome 258, *Nota di libri e scritture...*, Tome 39 of the '*Registri dei Decreti di Congregazione 1540–1566*, and '*Nota Decretorum Congregationis 1540–1604*'. Amounts in this and all other tables are in *scudi* and *baiocchi*. 1 *scudo* = 100 *baiocchi*. (The value of other coins could vary.) For 'certain' expenses, see the tables on rent and the wages of permanent employees. The degree of approximation of 'estimated' expenses is effectively larger only as regards loan losses (put at 200 *scudi* per year, i.e. around 5 per cent of the estimated total value of loans disbursed each year) and sundry expenses (10 per cent of all other expenses for the year). The pension assigned to Cosimo Ancaiano from 1546 onwards as reimbursement for the loss of benefits from the Ospedale dei Boemi is not included, as it is not certain whether it was actually paid each year in accordance with the terms of the agreement: the records of such payments only date back to late 1550s and the amounts are smaller than the originally agreed 200 *scudi*. There are no records of rental expense from 1546 onwards. Rent is assumed not to have changed from the latest available figure of sc. 21 b. 75 for the period comprising the second half of 1544 and the first half of 1545. The figures in italics for the years 1546–50 reflect this assumption, which is conservative; it is more likely that the Monte no longer paid rent after the merger with the Ospedale dei Boemi.

53 The transformation of the Monte from a 'free association of benefactors' into an arm of the papal administration would only become evident with the passage of time; it was not sanctioned by any official document.

54 According to the congregation's resolution of 16 June 1615, issued during the protectorate of Cardinal Aldobrandini, for loans exceeding that not inconsiderable amount borrowers paid 1 or 2 per cent interest.

55 Gregory XIII's decision was published in the brief *Inter multiplices* of 1 October 1584, cited in *Bolle e Privilegi del Sacro Monte della Pietà di Roma*, pp.61–4, and in M. Tosi, *op. cit.*, p.83. See, also, ASMP, '*Registro di Bolle, Brevi e Decreti di Congregazione*', Tome I, c.33. Legal deposits, generally made with notaries, were tied deposits made in connection with litigation pending or for other legal purposes. For the lifting of interest on small loans, see ASMP, '*Registri dei Decreti di Congregazione (1633–1643)*', Tome 45, c.62, relative to the congregation's meeting of 11 March 1636.

56 C.M. Travaglini, *op. cit.*, p. 466.

57 The Monte's importance to the local economy (See ASMP, Tome 258, *Nota di libri e scritture...*) can be gauged by its number of borrowers: between 25,000 and 26,000 out of a population of between 50,000 and 70,000. At the turn of the seventeenth century Camillo Fanucci of Siena (See C. Fanucci, *Trattato di tutte le Opere pie dell'alma città di Roma*, Rome, Stampatori Lepido Facili e Stefano Paolini, 1602) remarked on the

Monte's crucial role and observed that it made pledge loans of 'up to eight or ten *scudi* per person' for the term of a year. Fanucci must have been referring to contemporary practices, for his description contrasts with some of the rules adopted by the congregation in the mid-1580s.

58 See M. Tosi, *op. cit.*, p.191, for Benedict XIV's chirograph of 13 July 1743 and the obligations it imposed on the Monte.

II

THE MONTE DI PIETÀ OF ROME AS AN ECONOMIC AGENCY

The Monte's operations

The activities performed by the Monte

The Monte's principal activity was the granting of loans secured by pledges of valuables or movable goods for terms of between 3 and 6 months, usually renewable. The amounts were fairly small, generally between 2 and 3 *scudi*, and only one pledge loan per customer was permitted. Soon after its foundation other permissible activities were added. These 'accessory' activities included the safekeeping of valuables, deposit-taking, out-of-town money transfers on behalf of third parties, real estate administration and the acceptance and administration of trusts and bequests.

The lack of accounting documents for the Monte's early years precludes detailed description of the financial flows relating to pledge loans and comparison of their importance with that of the institution's ancillary operations. Some general references survive concerning the number of loans actually made per year and the amount of credit grantable to any one customer. Of particular interest are two resolutions that were adopted in 1565 on the management and administration of credit.[1] On 2 April a limit of 4 *scudi* of credit for every 6 *scudi* of collateral was fixed. Then, on 3 September, a ceiling of 3 *scudi* was set for lending to any one customer, even against multiple pledges. The aim of the latter resolution may well have been not so much to limit credit risk as to ensure that the Monte's assistance went to the needy, not to well-to-do opportunists seeking to take advantage of cheap credit for business or other purposes. On 19 August 1578 the loan limit per customer, which in the meantime had been raised to 6 *scudi*, was increased to 10; the rule of one pledge per customer remained in effect.[2] The ceiling on the size of loans that the loan officer could grant without specific authorisation from the congregation was raised from 3 to 5 *scudi* on 21 July 1580 and to 8 *scudi* on 4 April 1581. As early as 13 June of that year, however, it was lowered to 5 *scudi*, and on 10 October it was cut back to 3. On 30 January 1582 the ceiling of 6 *scudi* was reinstated. It is reasonable to suppose that the Monte, like similar institutions, initially concentrated on collateralised lending and engaged only marginally in other lines of business.[3]

Interests on deposits and reimbursement of expenses on loans

The need to raise cash probably first spurred the Monte to accept testamentary bequests and pecuniary deposits. It is likely that deposits at the Monte began to bear interest even before the official resolutions of 1552.[4] The congregation's resolution of 11 October 1569 ordering the return 'of the money being held at interest' is a significant subsequent clue.[5] While paying interest on deposits, at least up to 1552 the Monte charged no interest on loans, not even in the permissible form of reimbursement of expenses. The impression is that, before allowing that step to be taken, the Roman Curia tried in every feasible way to strengthen the institution's capital base, including merger with the Ospedale dei Boemi in 1546 and with the Company of San Bernardo in 1551. The fact that the Monte begin charging 5 per cent reimbursement in mid-1552 suggests that the effect of the latter merger had ceased by then, although there is no evidence of a demerger. Sizing up the persistent financial imbalance, on 4 April 1552 the congregation finally decided to begin requesting reimbursement of loan expenses. The resolution on the 'just' premium of 5 per cent was ratified on 30 May 1552 and the principle confirmed by the congregation in its meeting of 23 September 1569.[6] On 30 May 1552 the congregation, building on the practice of using private merchant companies as correspondents, decided to establish correspondence relationships with all the *monti di pietà* in Italy, thus reaffirming the Rome Monte's primacy.[7] These special correspondence relationships laid the foundation for the Monte's evolution into a banking institution and the linchpin of the credit system in the papal state.

Four years earlier, on 20 March 1548, the congregation had resolved to petition the pope for a general privilege, with the aim of obtaining favourable conditions for bequests made to the Monte and for customers' deposits, which were to be made transferable, and enabling the Rome Monte to extend these benefits and other indulgences to affiliated *monti* outside of Rome.[8] With the Jubilee of 1550 approaching, the congregation no doubt hoped to enable the Monte to compete with private bankers in handling pilgrims' remittances.[9] The desire to strengthen the

Fund-raising

Monte's ties with similar institutions may also have been a factor, both for reasons of ideals and in view of the lower costs involved in using a network of correspondents with a substantially different status from the private banks.

Fund-raising

Deposit transferability was a first indication of the need for a liquid instrument, i.e. one able to appeal to a substantial number of prospective providers of finance. The Monte could in any case borrow by means of the *cedole* that were proof of the deposit of sums of money and remained in use, and indeed grew in importance, even after the conferral of the Deposit Bank in 1584. Subsequently, it also raised funds by issuing *luoghi*, debt securities comparable to fixed-yield bonds. During the seventeenth century, as the Monte was increasingly absorbed into the public administration, these *luoghi* gradually became fully equivalent to public debt securities.[10]

The Monte began to take deposits of funds and goods early on, primarily to obtain the resources it needed for its ordinary activity: goods deposits were roughly comparable to today's safe-custody deposits; most cash deposits were remunerated in fine gold coin at an official and explicit rate of between 8 and 10 per cent, although some bore no interest.[11]

Donato Tamilia maintains that the Monte took deposits of cash and valuables practically from its inception, with the members of the Company implicitly assuming unlimited joint and several liability vis-à-vis depositors.[12] Other deposits were connected to trusts or testamentary bequests or dispositions. One of these, dated 24 June 1548, for 1000 *scudi* in the name of the Genoese merchant Giovanni Battista Libardi, envisaged a 'yield' (i.e. interest) of 100 *scudi* a year payable by the Monte.[13] This deposit was large enough to be brought to the attention of the congregation.

The extent to which the market actually regarded the Monte as a borrower belonging to the public sphere and its debt as sovereign debt can be gauged by comparing the Monte's deposit rates, as found in a limited number of observations, with the average rates on the public debt for the same period.

Despite the differences between Rome public debt securities[14] and the instruments issued by the Monte, which at first raised funds primarily through deposits and redeemable annuities, the market valued the Monte's debt on a par with the public debt.[15]

Table II *Annual interest payments and average interest rate on Rome public debt securities*[16]

Year	Pope	Annual interest on debt fund securities	Average interest rate
1552	Julius III	sc. 9,600	12.00%
1553	Julius III	sc. 17,000	10.00%
1554	Julius III	sc. 17,000	10.00%
1555	Paul IV	sc. 17,000	10.00%
1556	Paul IV	sc. 29,000	10.74%
1557	Paul IV	sc. 30,000	10.00%
1558	Paul IV	sc. 30,000	10.00%
1559	Pius IV	sc. 23,880	9.32%
1560	Pius IV	sc. 22,880	7.64%
1561	Pius IV	sc. 22,880	7.64%
1562	Pius IV	sc. 22,880	7.64%
1563	Pius IV	sc. 22,880	7.64%
1564	Pius IV	sc. 22,880	7.64%
1565	Pius IV	sc. 25,630	7.90%
1566	Pius V	sc. 25,630	7.90%
1567	Pius V	sc. 32,820	7.47%
1568	Pius V	sc. 31,242	7.23%
1569	Pius V	sc. 31,863	7.23%
1570	Pius V	sc. 31,436	7.23%
1571	Pius V	sc. 30,491	7.24%
1572	Gregory XIII	sc. 28,769	7.23%
1573	Gregory XIII	sc. 39,106	7.16%
1574	Gregory XIII	sc. 38,982	7.16%
1575	Gregory XIII	sc. 39,049	7.15%
1576	Gregory XIII	sc. 39,194	7.15%
1577	Gregory XIII	sc. 38,586	7.13%
1578	Gregory XIII	sc. 37,864	7.15%
1579	Gregory XIII	sc. 36,597	7.16%
1580	Gregory XIII	sc. 36,044	7.20%
1581	Gregory XIII	sc. 34,483	7.17%
1582	Gregory XIII	sc. 31,091	6.68%
1583	Gregory XIII	sc. 30,398	6.68%
1584	Gregory XIII	sc. 30,823	6.68%

Fund-raising

Table III *Deposits at the Monte di Pietà of Rome in its early years (1540–82)*[18]

Date	Period	Deposit	Interest	Depositor
22 May 1540	n/a	sc. 100		commitment of Rucellai
14 Jan. 1541	n/a	sc. 395 b. 75		A. Massimo (short-term)
7 May 1557	1556–7	sc. 1123 b. 28		D. Cobelli, Malta bishop
11 May 1559	11 May– 7 Sep.1559	sc. 230		M. Mosca (long-term)
9 Sep. 1560	Sep.1560– Mar.1561	sc. 350 gold	sc. 14 gold	Caterina Fiamega
27 Jan. 1561	from 4 Feb. 1561	sc. 800	8% p.a.	n/a
2 Mar. 1562	1562–3	sc. 1106		Carlo Fausto Orsini[19]
15 June 1562	1562	sc. 100	sc. 10	Abbess of S. John[20]
4 Oct. 1563	n/a	sc. 900		n/a
30 May 1566	n/a	sc. 1000	8% p.a.	n/a
18 June 1567	n/a	sc. 700	sc. 350	n/a[21]
10 Nov. 1567	annuity	sc. 100	20% p.a.	n/a[22]
16 June 1573	1 year	sc. 100		A. Ciampoli (surety deposit)
23 June 1573	n/a	sc. 152	sc. 7½	Tiberio de Marsianis
8 Feb. 1575	annuity	sc. 2000	10.5% p.a.	n/a
6 Feb. 1582	n/a	sc. 2000		cashier's surety deposit
Total		**sc. 10,807 b. 3** **sc. 350 gold**	**sc. 367½** **sc. 14 gold**	

Note: n/a = not available (applies to all tables)

The resolutions passed by the congregation in the mid-1560s laid down that deposits were to bear interest of between 6 and 9 per cent, with an average rate of around 8 per cent. The terms of the few transactions whose records survive accord with these guidelines. In other words, these were not dead-letter resolutions.[17] The Monte probably began to raise funds through issues of *luoghi* in the early 1570s. It is uncertain whether the first *luoghi* were similar to the securities that the Monte used widely in the seventeenth century. On 25 May 1574 a general meeting of the congregation ratified the decision of a select congregation (i.e. a management committee) for eight bond issues and on 20 August 1580 the Monte issued 4000 *scudi* of new *luoghi*.

Not all of the institution's debt was at market rates. Bequests and testamentary dispositions were an important source of new capital, as were donations and alms, the flow of which was encouraged by special privileges. From 1553, for example, permission was given for a collection box for donations to the Monte to be kept permanently in the principal churches of Rome.[23]

The link with government

Although it was not until 1584 that Pope Gregory XIII officially appointed the Monte depositary of security for lawsuits and legal proceedings, the institution had evidently begun to perform that function much earlier. On 25 May 1574 Gregory XIII ordered the establishment of a depository for pledges and goods subject to execution in connection with judicial proceedings and entrusted it to the Monte. On 31 January 1581 the congregation decided that the Monte could cover the depository's financial needs upon authorisation of the viscount-judge.[24]

On 6 March 1582 the Monte received a request from the Apostolic Chamber that it deposit with the papal depositary all its 'idle' cash on hand. This is reminiscent of modern-day moves to adjust public finances by requiring social security institutions or other public bodies to deposit their funds with the treasury or even to invest some of them in government debt securities. The Monte may have been able to avoid complying, for in the same meeting of 6 March it was decided to discuss the matter with the treasurer. Certainly, if the definition of free funds was actually left to the treasurer, who was a banker, it is not improbable that no action was taken. The Monte's status as a quasi-public entity was soon made official. On 1 October 1584, with the brief *Inter multiplices*, Gregory XIII entrusted the Deposit Bank to the Monte, thereby transforming the latter into the equivalent of a state bank.

The accounts of the Deposit Bank in its first year of activity

The Deposit Bank began operating soon after the papal brief was published. The title page of its first ledger reads:[25]

In the name of the Lord God, Amen

The accounts of the Deposit Bank in its first year of activity

Ledger of the Sacro Monte di Pietà of Rome in which will be entered all the deposits made up to the day in this Monte, both by virtue of the brief granted by Our Most Holy Lord Pope Gregory XIII on the first of October of this year 1584 and for whatsoever other reason and cause incumbent on the present provvisori of said Monte:

L'Ill.mo Henricho Caetano

Il Sr. Stefano Crescentio

Il Sr. Giovanni Enriquez

The first accounting period formally opened on 1 October 1584 and concluded on 20 September 1585. Although the first three months of activity were purely nominal (the first statement of accounts entered in the ledger is dated 1 January 1585), it was decided, perhaps a posteriori, to close the accounts exactly one year after the promulgation of the papal brief and to adopt a financial year commencing 1 October thereafter.

The date of the first statement of accounts and the ledger's heading of 1585 suggest that the original plan was for the financial year to coincide with the calendar year. The first annual accounts of the Deposit Bank closed with a deficit of around 1790 *scudi*, probably corresponding to interest payable on deposits, administrative and operating expenses and start-up costs.

Although they provide plentiful information on the Deposit Bank, these ledgers give us a partial view of the Monte's activities, omitting pledge loans and other operations. In addition, they are sometimes hard to interpret, because they were prepared in the same manner as the accounting records that merchants made for their private companies. Quite possibly they were drawn up by employees of merchants who held office as depositary or treasurer at the Monte or even by the merchants themselves.

The entries are highly detailed and refer to individual deposit or loan transactions, occasionally grouped by type, date or authorising officer (a *deputato* or *provvisore*). It was standard practice, sanctioned by several resolutions of the congregation, never to lend against multiple pledges or to accept more than one pledge per person. Barring exceptions, this rules out the presence of multiple accounts, i.e. more than one transaction with the same counter-party, which are frequent in the books of the merchant companies.

Despite these limitations, the summary accounts give us insight into the Monte's position in the economy of Rome in the

Table IV *Cumulative balances of deposits for judicial proceedings at the Monte di Pietà of Rome: first financial year (1 October 1584 – 30 September 1585)*[27]

Date	Receipts (cumulative)	Disbursements (cumulative)
1 Oct. 1584	n/a	n/a
1 Jan. 1585	sc. 1635 b. 59½	sc. 1970 b. 41½
26 Jan. 1585	sc. 3203 b. 90½	sc. 3844 b. 52½
23 Mar. 1585	sc. 5742 b. 95	sc. 6763 b. 17½
2 May 1585	sc. 7060 b. 54½	sc. 8315 b. 16½
21 May 1585	sc. 7669 b. 99½	sc. 9018 b. 93½
29 May 1585	sc. 8432 b. 61½	sc. 9770 b. 97
12 June 1585	sc. 10,756 b. 41½	sc. 11,175 b. 97
9 July 1585	sc. 11,701 b. 10	sc. 13,064 b. 32
8 Aug. 1585	sc. 12,935 b. 45	sc. 14,336 b. 03
27 Aug. 1585	sc. 18,235 b. 43	sc. 19,072 b. 52
30 Sep. 1585	sc. 22,100 b. 02	sc. 23,890 b. 40¼
3 Oct. 1585 (deficit, financial year)	(sc. 1790 b. 98)	

late sixteenth century and provide transaction details that shed light on the institution's ordinary customer base.

Other activities

The Monte carried on other activities beside its core business from its very first years. Some of these services were closely related to its institutional purposes, e.g. the remittance of funds to correspondents (usually other *monti*), others more typical of traditional banking proper, e.g. deposits, safe deposit, perhaps foreign exchange.[26] Some transactions carried out or authorised by the administration of the Monte between the years 1541 and 1582 are shown in Table V.

The entries in the source documents refer in particular to expenses connected with events dating back to the Monte's first decade of life, such as the payments to the notary who drew up the document for the merger of the Monte with the Ospedale dei Boemi – these payments were probably disputed, given the delay with which they were authorised – and legal expenses for litigation pending, such as the action brought against Angelo Raimondi in the early 1560s.

References to investments are almost entirely lacking, although the Monte's capital may well have been employed in

Table v *Payments and funds transfers between the Monte and third parties or customers, 1541–82* [30]

	Period	Amount	Counter-party
4 Dec. 1542	13 Nov. 1541	sc. 28 b. 78	Agostino Pessina, custodian of the Monte
28 July 1557	short-term	sc. 7 b. 50	dowry of Maddalena di Zanobio[31]
8 May 1560	short-term	sc. 18	F.C. de Galosio, notary[32]
17 July 1560	part of 1560	sc. 82 b. 50	pension to Cosimo Ancaiano
14 Oct. 1560	1560	sc. 10 gold	Fra Marturino, convent of S.Trinità[33]
17 Feb. 1561	1560–1	sc. 24 b. 50	various workers[34]
4 July 1561	part of 1561	sc. 82 b. 50	pension to Cosimo Ancaiano
4 July 1561	short-term	sc. 18	F.C. de Galosio, notary
1 Mar. 1573	short-term	sc. 1400	settlement with Lodovico Lante
21 July 1579	short-term	sc. 125	Isabella Papi[35]
5 July 1582	short-term	sc. 150	'Pilgrim' (monastery of San P.)
Total		**sc. 1936 b.78 + sc. 10 gold**	

operations other than pledge loans. One indication is the decision of the congregation on 13 January 1573 to invest idle funds in bonds issued by the Monte della Carne.[28] This could not have been a long-term investment, since the debt fund in question was extinguished that same year. The dearth of references in Tome 39 of the *Registri dei Decreti di Congregazione, 1540–1566* is explained by the fact that entries in the second part of the volume were occasional, not continuous, and were limited to transactions important enough to be annotated as reference for the deliberations and decisions of the board.

Nonetheless, a reasonable estimate can be made of how much money the Monte had to raise in the market. Fixed costs ranged between 400 and 500 *scudi* a year up to perhaps 1560.[29] With some 3000 *scudi* a year needed to finance lending, the total requirement came to around 3500 *scudi* a year at least for the period

1545–60.[36] This can be measured against total public debt in Rome, since the debt issued by the Monte di Pietà was of comparable quality and carried similar conditions.[37] Bearing in mind that government borrowing through the various public *monti* represented only part, albeit a large one, of total borrowing in the market, the new entrant's modest impact on the total stock of debt outstanding is evidenced by Table VI.[38]

That the Monte's activity was not limited to pawnbroking is confirmed by the matters addressed in several resolutions of the congregation, among them that of 20 March 1548, and, indirectly, by the fact that prominent bankers and merchants, from families such as the Rucellai, Calciati, Crivelli, Massimo and Diaz, served in the congregation in various capacities. It was fairly common for the members of the congregation or their representatives to guarantee jointly and severally the obligations that the Monte contracted. The surety deposits made by members or officers of the Company appear to have been a means of providing financial support.[39] All this indicates activity that may have extended to deposits and transactions involving banks or merchant companies managed by men who had a fiduciary relationship with the institution. In the congregation's meeting of 13 January 1541, for example, Luigi Rucellai, a prominent merchant and authoritative member of the congregation, received solemn confirmation of the Monte's obligations to him for the funds he had advanced in order to meet payments. The summary of the congregation's meeting of 2 May 1541, where Fra Giovanni of Calvi, the Monte's founder, brought donations of 500 *scudi* from the King of Portugal and 100 from the Duke of Calabria, the heir to the throne, mentions that these funds were transferred by a *cedula cambii* (bill of exchange) drawn on Rome. In the meeting of 2 March 1544 Fra Giovanni prohibited accepting promises of alms (it is uncertain whether he was referring to written commitments, hence to 'securities' comparable to *cedole*), given the difficulties that had arisen in similar cases even vis-à-vis prelates.

Borrowing money was evidently a fixture of treasury management operations. But whereas the Monte rather seldom had recourse to direct loans, it frequently accepted testamentary legacies whereby it undertook to pay a life or redeemable annuity in exchange for a one-off deposit of capital.[40] Given the form of these transactions, which explicitly mentioned the percentage of the capital corresponding to the annuity, like the coupon of a security, testamentary legacies were the form of fund-raising most closely resembling the taking out of a loan. Operations of this

Table VI *Total end-year stock of Roman public debt securities outstanding*[41]

	Pope	Total nominal capital (sc.)	Number of public debt funds active
1552	Julius III	80,000	1
1553	Julius III	170,000	1
1554	Julius III	170,000	1
1555	Paul IV	170,000	1
1556	Paul IV	270,000	2
1557	Paul IV	300,000	2
1558	Paul IV	300,000	2
1559	Pius IV	256,000	2
1560	Pius IV	299,333	2
1561	Pius IV	299,333	2
1562	Pius IV	299,333	2
1563	Pius IV	299,333	2
1564	Pius IV	299,333	2
1565	Pius IV	324,333	3
1566	Pius V	324,333	3
1567	Pius V	439,333	4
1568	Pius V	432,033	4
1569	Pius V	440,900	5
1570	Pius V	434,800	6
1571	Pius V	421,300	6
1572	Gregory XIII	397,900	6
1573	Gregory XIII	545,800	8
1574	Gregory XIII	544,300	8
1575	Gregory XIII	545,900	8
1576	Gregory XIII	548,200	9
1577	Gregory XIII	540,800	9
1578	Gregory XIII	529,200	9
1579	Gregory XIII	511,100	9
1580	Gregory XIII	500,000	9
1581	Gregory XIII	481,000	9
1582	Gregory XIII	465,300	9
1583	Gregory XIII	455,000	9
1584	Gregory XIII	461,100	8

Table VII *Rent payments to Gian Pietro Crivelli for business offices of the Monte di Pietà of Rome, 1539–45*[48]

Date	Period	Amount paid
n/a	2nd half 1539–1st half 1540	sc. 22 b. 87½ (?)
8 Aug. 1541	2nd half 1540–1st half 1541	sc. 22 b. 87½
3 Oct. 1541	2nd half 1541–1st half 1542	sc. 22 b. 87½
8 Oct. 1542	2nd half 1542	sc. 10 b. 87½
30 Mar. 1543	1st half 1543	sc. 12 b. 87½
n/a	2nd half 1543–1st half 1544	sc. 21¾ (?)
n/a	2nd half 1544–1st half 1545	sc. 21¾ (?)
Total	1539–45 (estimated)	**sc. 135 b. 87½**

kind were common among *monti di pietà* in general.[42] They were not without risk. The meeting of the congregation of 8 May 1572 called on the cashier collecting a legacy to be 'certain it is paid in as such to the Monte'.[43] Plainly, there had been cases of insolvency on the part of those who had committed funds to the Monte (bringing to mind Fra Giovanni's warning against 'promises of alms').

Buildings

The congregation also frequently dealt with the administration of the Monte's buildings. Whether these were rented to third parties or served instead as business premises or dwellings for prominent important members of the Company, the picture that emerges from the documentation is one of operations not unlike those of a modern public agency.

In its first years the Monte rented the building in which its offices were housed from Gian Pietro Crivelli, one of its founders. The building was located 'in the place called the Chiavica opposite the Church of Santa Lucia' near Crivelli's shop.[44] Crivelli had probably rented the building to the Monte as early as 2 April 1539, the date on which the Monte presumably began to operate, although the lease runs from 3 June of that year.[45]

From 1504 the Crivelli family had paid rent of 42 *scudi* a year to the Ospedale dei Boemi in Rome for a perpetual lease to a building serving as both goldsmith's shop and residence.[46] Crivelli, who later lived at 22 Via dei Banchi Vecchi, not far from the building into which the Monte had moved, was assessed as an inhabitant of the Ponte quarter of Rome in 1504 and was mentioned among the goldsmiths of Rome in 1508.[47] He died on

14 June 1552, having served as a *provvisore* of the Monte in 1551. His son Giovanni Angelo, who also held office as *provvisore*, in 1560, at some point became embroiled in litigation with the Monte over a question of rent payments, possibly for the same building.[49]

The Monte's first offices were in the immediate vicinity of the main building of the Ospedale dei Boemi, the 'house with a tower', where the deposit of pledge goods was located for years following the merger.[50] Rent would appear to have been paid every six months. The four entries in the surviving records refer only to the period up to 1543 and typically read:

> By order of the *provvisori* of the Monte della Pietà, you Messer Francesco Calciati, are commanded to pay to Messer Gian Pietro Crivello for the rent of the Monte's house 22 *scudi* and 87½ *baiocchi* for which you will obtain a receipt and which you will enter in the Monte's account.[51]

The rent may be assumed to have remained unchanged up to the merger in 1546, after which the charge logically should have ceased to exist. The Monte had its headquarters at the Ospedale dei Boemi until 25 June 1567, when the congregation approved a proposal to rent Palazzo Orsini, near Piazza Catinara, as the head office for 89 *scudi* a year.[52]

In 1579 the Monte moved to a building of the College of Jesuits, near what is today Via dell'Ara Coeli. Five years later it returned to the building in Piazza Catinara, but only briefly, for in 1585 it moved again, this time to the vicinity of the church of San Salvatore in Lauro. Finally, at the end of 1603, the Monte moved into what would be its permanent headquarters in the former Santacroce-Petrignani palace.[53]

The congregation's agenda often included matters relating to the Monte's real estate holdings, which had become very substantial following the merger with the Ospedale dei Boemi. On 4 July 1558, for example, the congregation discussed the house rented for life to Orazio di Nicolò da Urbino, who in renouncing his right asked for a form of compensation. The house was again available to the Monte on 6 August 1558. The question seems to have been drawn out, for only on 14 November 1560 did the congregation authorise a 'settlement' concerning the house 'that was Nicolò da Urbino's'.[54] The meeting of 27 July 1558 was devoted almost exclusively to the requests of Quirino Garrone regarding the house leased to him by the Monte. The meeting of 3 February 1562 decided to rent the house at

Sant'Eustacchio that had been Domenico Crescenzi's for 100 gold *scudi*; the substantial sum indicates either that the building was large or that the contract was not really a lease proper but concerned an annuity or life interest. On 5 July 1563 the delegates turned their attention to a house of Crivelli's (probably not the one near the church of Santa Lucia) that had been donated to the Monte and reviewed the relations between the Monte and the tenants. On 26 February 1567 they discussed finding a buyer for the house owned by the former cashier, Diego Algeziro, and calling on one Caterina Lodovisi to repair the house she leased to the Monte. On 5 January 1568 the congregation decided to put up for sale the house that had belonged to the late Francesco Bacconi.

A curious 'case' dates from mid-1562. On 2 April of that year the congregation ordered that the houses near the Monte's head office should be rented, owing to the 'reduction in the rents' of the buildings owned by the Monte, but in their next meeting, on 27 April, the delegates took note of the cause of that reduction and resolved to bring action 'against the custodian who prevented the leasing of the Monte's properties'.[55] There was no follow-up, however, for on 4 May we find that 'the custodian asks for forgiveness and obtains it'.[56]

The settlement of the question of the Ospedale dei Boemi also proved to be protracted. In 1580 the congregation directed the committee entrusted with handling the dispute to demand 785 gold *scudi* 'for the question of the Ospedale', which by a papal decretal of 1572 had been demerged from the Monte and returned to the original owners. The vicissitudes of the relationship between the Monte and the Ospedale testify to the important influence of the papal government on the Monte's growth, which was paralleled by the Monte's taking over functions that had previously been discharged by organs of the apostolic administration.

Lending and pawnbroking: scope and procedures

The Monte's credit activity, 1539–84

The Monte's actual operations commenced with a number of pledge loans dating from 2 April 1539 onwards, that is to say before the papal bull *Ad Sacram Beati Petri Sedem* officially sanctioning its foundation was issued on 9 September.[57] As mentioned, its first headquarters were the shop and accompanying house that Gian Pietro Crivelli had made available near the church of Santa Lucia alla Chiavica.

The initial stock of capital was rather modest, amounting to only 894 *scudi* and 40 *baiocchi*, partly lent out and partly held in cash.[58] Activity in the first year was relatively limited, consisting of a total of 729 pledge loans[59] granted for amounts of presumably between 1 and 3 *scudi* and for an average term of around 6 months.[60] This suggests that loan disbursements in 1539 amounted to between 1200 and 1500 *scudi*, a figure that accords with the Monte's initial capital of just under 900 *scudi*, considering the possibility that the same funds could be lent out more than once (bad debts permitting). It is also likely that alms and donations had in the meantime increased the available stock of capital. With the passage of time, it became customary for each member of the Company to contribute 2 *carlini* a year. The number of loans rose to 2643 in 1540 and then held more or less steady at around 2500 a year until 1550, when it increased to 2943.[61] This would indicate an average annual volume of lending of between 4000 and 5000 *scudi*. Since loans were for terms of six months, taking account of losses and bad debts, the average amount of capital employed by the Monte in credit activity can be estimated at between 3000 and 3500 *scudi*.

Growth and credit risk

The weight of expired and unredeemed pledges, bad debts and losses arising in the operation of the warehouse for pledged goods must have been rather substantial throughout the early period of activity. The difficulties are reflected in the summary record of the first meeting of the 'special committee' set up in 1556 by the protector, Rodolfo Pio di Carpi. Much of the discussion at that meeting, held on 16 August in the cloister of San Girolamo alla Regola, concerned the restructuring of the Monte's creditor positions, which surely included a large number of non-performing items.[62] In fact, it was decided to renegotiate all loans in default except for the considerable amount owed by the keeper of pledges, Agostino Pessina. It was also decided to estimate the hypothetical losses that would be incurred in the event that the pledges were sold at auction, i.e. to calculate the estimated realisable value of the pledged assets backing up positions in default.

Notwithstanding the difficulties, operations continued to expand. Although there are no specific data on the scale of activity between 1550 and 1580, volumes must have grown slowly but steadily until the end of the 1570s. The same sources of information on the scale of operations up to 1550 also contain some figures relating to the early 1580s.[63] The number of loans rose appreciably compared with the years 1540 to 1550, averaging about 15,000 a year between 1580 and 1585. In 1580 a total of 15,570 loan contracts were concluded; the number of pledges accepted – as noted, according to the Statutes, only one loan per pledge was permitted – totalled 13,543 in 1584 and rose to 16,267 the next year. Lending activity continued to expand after the conferral of the Bank of Deposits for Judicial Proceedings in 1584, with new loan contracts leaping to 25,609 by 1589. The sources do not contain specific references to significant lending activity other than pledge loans or a few deposits during the Monte's first years.[64] Unfortunately, no ledgers, balance sheets or other primary sources documenting the overall volume of business generated by the Monte's credit activity are to be found in the archives.

The estimate given in Table VIII is therefore based on the single, fairly continuous time series available for the period from the foundation to the end of the sixteenth century, namely the number of pledge loans made per year. The raw data are contained in Gabrielli's summary, which dates back to 1603 and also mentions the presence at the Monte of a series of now lost registers regarding the Monte's accounts and the inventories of the depository for pledges. The estimate is based on a hard fact, the annual number of loans, and an arbitrary hypothesis, the average loan amount, reflecting general information drawn from other available sources, particularly the resolutions adopted by the congregation, which from time to time set stringent limits on how much money could be lent to any one borrower. Usually the ceiling was rather low, presumably less than 3 *scudi*, but at times it was raised, albeit briefly, to 8 and even 10 *scudi*. The hypothesis adopted is that the average annual value was equal to half the ceiling in force, where this is known; where the ceiling is not known, the average annual value is set equal to that for the closest years for which the ceiling is known.

As to the amount of working capital the Monte required, let us recall that the Statutes of 1565 established a loan limit of 3 *scudi* for a term of six months. If we take 2 *scudi* as approximating the 'average' loan, the working capital employed by the Monte was on the order of 15,000–20,000 *scudi*, after adjustment for bad debts, losses and operating expenses. Since the population of Rome at the time can plausibly be estimated at between 50,000

Table VIII *Estimate of the Monte's total lending activity, 1539–84* [65]

Year(s)	Number of transactions	Average amount (sc.)	Total amount (sc.)
1539	729	1½	1093½
1540	2643	1½	3964½
1541–2	n/a	1½	n/a
1543	2869	1½	4303½
1544–9	n/a	1½	n/a
1550	2943	1½	4414½
1551	3837	1½	5755½
1552–5	n/a	1½	n/a
1556	6576	1½	9864
1557–8	n/a	1½	n/a
1559	2437	1½	3655½
1560	3120	1½	4680
1561	3907	1½	5860½
1562	2478	1½	3717
1563	3614	1½	5421
1564	4450	1½	6675
1565	4782	1½	7173
1566	7266	1½	10,899
1567	7486	1½	11,229
1568	8257	1½	12,385½
1569	6842	1½	10,263
1570	6014	1½	9021
1571	6629	1½	9943½
1572	8584	1½	12,876
1573	12,705	2	25,410
1574	12,142	2	24,284
1575	12,898	2	25,796
1576	13,850	2	27,700
1577	13,176	2	26,352
1578	12,508	2	25,016
1579	14,111	2	28,222
1580	15,470	2	30,940
1581	13,749	2¾	37,809¾
1582	12,860	3	38,580
1583	14,351	3	43,053
1584	13,543	3	40,629
Total[66]	256,826		sc. 516,986 b. 25

and 60,000, a figure of 15,000 loans a year – considered as separate transactions since there are no grounds for thinking that the rule of 'one pledge per loan and per person' had been amended at that time – points to an average of between 5,000 and 7,500 customers a year, equal to between 10 and 15 per cent of the resident population. (Of course, loans could also have been made to residents of the surrounding countryside or to foreigners.)

This would indicate that the Monte held a truly pre-eminent position in the loan market in Rome in the late sixteenth century, at least in terms of 'market penetration', but such a conclusion must be weighed against the composition of the Monte's customer base, made up primarily of the needy and the working classes. Guilds such as the barbers, shoemakers, smiths and others had supported the Monte, as testified to by the offers presented in May 1552, and so it is logical to suppose that their members had a stake in its future as a going concern. Petty craftsmen and tradesmen may have turned to the Monte to finance small outlays or to cover occasional shortfalls of cash, of the kind that routinely occur even in economically sound and profitable businesses.

This apparently contradicts the conventional notion that artisans only turned to the Monte when business was bad. One possible explanation lies in the extraordinary reach and ramification of the Monte's operations in Rome.

Interest, lending and collateral

The first years were not easy, however. Until 1552 the Monte's pledge loans carried no interest, not even in the form of reimbursement of expenses that the Fifth Lateran Council had approved in 1515.[67] Not until mid-1552, probably following a persistent financial shortfall, did the Monte begin to demand the 5 per cent margin that was deemed to be 'just'.[68] The policy was formally adopted on 30 May 1552 and subsequently confirmed by the congregation on 23 September 1569. Meanwhile, regular, explicit interest was paid on deposits, although in most cases the contract with the depositor was not a proper deposit contract but took the form of a testamentary 'bequest', which involved fewer formal impediments to the remuneration of capital. On 23 March 1579, however, the *provvisori*, acting on precise instructions of the protector, Cardinal Francesco Alciati, ordered that the payment of interest on deposits be suspended.[69]

Pledge loan activity was broadly in line with the model announced in the founding bull.[70] The loans were usually small,

Interest, lending and collateral

secured by movable goods (often jewellery or furnishings) and at short term (3 to 6 months, usually renewable), and it was the practice not to grant more than one loan, secured by a single pledge, to each borrower. Appraisal of collateral preceded disbursement. From the Monte's first years, lending was transacted on Monday and Friday, with at least two delegates always present.

On 30 August 1563 it was decided to hold auctions regularly on Wednesday. The appraiser was directed to 'book' the prices of the goods sold next to the valuations that had made at the time of their acceptance. Unfortunately, there is no surviving trace of these entries.[71]

The need to verify the appraisals shows that the adequacy of collateral in relation to disbursements was a problem. The absence, at least in the first years, of specific resolutions on the relation of appraisal value to credit disbursement reflects what was probably a rough-and-ready approach to lending and helps to explain the ensuing losses. Indirect references to the latter crop up in recurring resolutions on the keeping of the warehouse, the responsibility of the Monte's officials and the sisable surety deposits some of them had to make.

More generally, however, the Monte's loan losses can be attributed to a multiplicity of causes, notable among which was the decision to make lending procedures as favourable as possible to the most indigent borrowers. Borrowers could redeem their goods for a term of six months. Only if a borrower defaulted would the item he had pledged be put up for sale at the next auction. If the proceeds of the sale exceeded the amount of the loan, the difference, following the extinguishing of all obligations, went to the insolvent debtor.[72] This general rule, inspired by the founding bull, was never amended despite the many provisions that the congregation issued in subsequent decades concerning auctions and the collection of the items purchased. For example, on 22 November 1569 the congregation decided that an object not paid for and collected by the buyer within fifteen days could be sold to another person; any down payment by the first buyer would be considered lost.[73] Less than a year later, on 17 October 1570, the delegates decided instead that if a buyer failed to pay the purchase price within the time limit (set by discretion and thus not necessarily the fifteenth day following the auction), the original owner could regain possession by paying an amount equal not to purchase price but to the valuation set by the appraiser.[74]

The participation of Monte officials in auctions was another issue of long debate. On 9 February 1568 the congregation decided that only the appointed delegate and no one else could make a bid during an auction. As early as 7 June 1569, however, it determined that 'no official, neither for himself nor for the Monte, in whatsoever case, nor for third parties, may or shall buy or bid on pledges of the Monte when these are sold'.[75] The matter came up again on 23 March 1574, but this time it was decided that all officials could attend auctions and buy for cash or future payment. Such purchases were subject to a limitation: for 'the space of one month' the Monte would set the object aside for the original owner, who could redeem it by paying the same amount as the winning bid. This decision recalls the resolution adopted in the Monte's infancy, on 11 May 1540, under Cardinal Quinones, but the earlier rule was applicable to all purchasers, not just members of the Company. In the event, other amendments followed, and on 8 April 1578 the congregation laid down that officers or employees could bid only in their own name and prohibited them from buying or bidding on behalf of others.

The regulation of sales was the object of frequent discussion and decisions that were incorporated into successive versions of the Statutes. For example, on 20 November 1559 the congregation laid down that loans would not be made on Fridays barring specific authorisation and that pledges were only to be sold with the approval and in the presence of at least two delegates. On 26 January 1574 it determined that auctions should take place in the presence of at least one delegate. Both decisions sanctioned a long-standing practice.[76] On 16 March 1574 it was decided to hold auctions every Monday.

Much attention was also paid to the organisation of lending and other operations. On 2 April 1567 the congregation ruled that loans should be made on Tuesdays and Fridays, after lunch, and scheduled its own meetings for Tuesdays at 11 a.m. On 5 May 1573 it decided that ordinary activity would be taken care of on weekdays, from daylight until noon, leaving officers and employees free the rest of the day. Monday, being auction day, was an exception. Decisions of this kind often came in swift succession. On 8 February and 15 March 1575 the congregation decided that during Lent its meetings would be held after lunch and that 'lending and collection shall likewise take place after lunch, except for Monday morning'. Collection was permitted on Monday up to 'sermon time'. The schedule was again changed on 31 October 1575, so that 'collecting, pledging and

Interest, lending and collateral

lending is to take place every day and the officers and employees are to turn out at sunrise and stay five consecutive hours until the end of April next'. On 22 December 1579, referring to a transaction, the congregation decreed that appraisals and sales must take place at the Monte's premises.

Earlier, on 2 March 1558, it was decided to affix notices in the streets of Rome announcing the dates of the next auctions. This set a precedent, since in subsequent meetings (11 November 1559, 2 September 1560, 14 August 1564 and 12 November 1565) the congregation authorised public announcement of the sale of unredeemed pledges. Meanwhile, the Monte persisted in endeavouring to weave a protectionist web around its auctions, not least by urging the public authorities in Rome and beyond to prohibit simultaneous or rival auctions.[77] On 9 December 1570 the congregation voted to accompany the announcement of an auction with a warning to others not to hold similar events before or during that of the Monte. On that occasion it also decided to allow customers whose tickets had not expired to sell their goods at auction.

Auctions were often the focus of discussions with the Jewish moneylenders. On 14 May 1565, for example, the congregation examined the question of competing auctions and the acceptance of sub-deposits of collateral from the Jewish lenders. And on 15 February 1568 it prohibited the cashier from issuing certificates attesting to deposits made by Jews in connection with irregular financial operations (*'circa la trasgressione degli hebrei'*).

As to the administration of the goods that had been pawned, the congregation frequently had to delve into the details of loans or to define the mandates of Monte officials with regard to procedural matters and security. On 19 March 1567 it debated whether or not the Monte could accept pledges of fabric having an ornamental border in silver or gold on a silk base, no doubt in light of the risk of fraud or deterioration. On 1 December of the same year it decided that 'gold, pearls, silver, rings and the like must be pledged separately from other things such as linen cloth, wool, cauldrons and other furniture'. On 26 January 1568 it established that the proceeds of the sale of goods had to be kept 'in a separate place', with same-day reconciliation of accounts. In addition, when a loan was made, an entry was to be made under disbursements and the depositary notified. On 3 February 1568 the congregation reiterated that the accountant and the cashier always had to be able to enter the 'loan room'.[78] On 29 December 1567 the congregation ordered a general audit of the depository of pledged goods. On 22 June 1568 it gave instructions for an inventory of new pledges be taken at least once a week and for the keeper to receive 10 *carlini* for that purpose. On 11 August 1568 three delegates were appointed, one responsible for supervising sales, the second for lending and the third for collecting the sums payable. On 26 August 1575 the rules for the sale of jewels and diamonds were decided: 'The keeper shall take them to the provvisori, and at least one of them with one of you delegates shall show them secretly to the appraisers, and one of these must later attend the sale'. Considering the tenor of these instructions, it is not unlikely that there had been cases of fraud. On 6 September 1575 the congregation acknowledged that a receipt had been given to the keeper for a pledged item that he had delivered to the deputy protector and it instructed the accountant to mention this in the note referring to that pledge. An important resolution was adopted on 17 April 1584, when the congregation decided that unexpired pledges, which could be sold only at the request of the owner, were to be included alongside expired pledges in regular auctions.

The Monte's increasing size and importance were both cause and effect of its slow transition from charitable institution to state entity. As noted, a key step in this process was Pope Gregory XIII's brief of 25 May 1574 ordering the establishment of a depository for pledges and goods subject to execution in connection with judicial proceedings and entrusting it to the Monte.[79] With the papacy of Gregory XIII, and particularly with the conferral of the Bank of Deposits in 1584, pawnbroking, though remaining important to the Monte and part of its mission, was most likely no longer its core business.

Administrative control and managerial powers

The organisational structure of administration

The Monte's organisational structure, which had not been clearly defined at the beginning, changed constantly in the early years. From the start its central organ was the congregation, the meeting of the delegates of the Company, normally chaired by the cardinal-protector or, in his absence, by a vicar or a designated prelate. This appears to have been the only operational function of the cardinal-protector, whose role was principally to set broad policy lines for the institution's activity. Any comparison with the role of chairman of the board in a modern bank must take the protector's high ecclesiastic rank into account, for the founding bull, perhaps partly to underscore the primacy bestowed on the new institution among all *monti di pietà*, designated the cardinal-protector of the Franciscans to perform the same function in the Monte di Pietà of Rome.

The congregation remained pivotal in setting administrative policy until 1557, when the first official statutes assigned many of its tasks to a smaller 'special committee', which still had to submit its own decisions to the congregation for ratification. Besides voting on general matters in meetings of the congregation, the delegates were also involved in day-to-day operations: at least two of them had to be present at the time goods were consigned and loans disbursed. The first organisational plan provided for a somewhat vague general delegation of power to two *provvisori* responsible for overseeing ordinary operations. Three delegates were to be entrusted with accounting and administrative controls and keeping the accounts, another, called the depositary or treasurer, was to be made responsible for cash and valuables, and a secretary was to draw up the minutes of the congregation's meetings. The congregation officially adopted this structure on 11 April 1540.[80] It designated three delegates (Massimo, Rucellai and Calciati) to keep the accounts and one (Calciati) to be treasurer until the end of 1540, named Antonio Lomellino and Giacomo Crescenzi *provvisori* for the next three months, elected Gian Giacomo Tassi as secretary (Tassi also served as accountant) and made Angelo Antonio Tasca 'cashier', that is to say keeper of the strongbox. Tasca would remain in office until his death on 2 March 1547.

In the early years it was customary to appoint the *provvisori* for three-month terms, but *provvisori* often remained in office longer because of the long intervals between meetings of the congregation. On 10 May 1540 the congregation assigned Giacomo Crescenzi to oversee the valuation of goods to be pawned, thus creating the office of appraiser.[81] The administrative structure was first modified during the first meeting of the congregation chaired by Cardinal Pio di Carpi on 13 January 1541, which designated new *provvisori* for three months and a depositary (Francesco Calciati), and delegated Girolamo Boccaurato and Luigi Rucellai to audit the accounts.[82] The auditors' powers were limited to checking the performance of the depositary. The latter had more extensive functions, combining those of treasurer with the duties originally entrusted to the accountant. These two offices remained coupled for a decade, until the merger with the Company of San Bernardo.

The desire of Cardinal Pio di Carpi to mould an efficient and soundly structured institution was certainly a factor in the round of organisational changes introduced in 1541. On 29 March[83] and in a series of ensuing meetings, the congregation began to establish the administrative and operational rules that would gradually be transformed from standard practice into arrangements enshrined in the Statutes. To begin with, the congregation made it compulsory for *provvisori* to designate a deputy or alternate in the event of prolonged absence, and decided that two delegates would be appointed as guarantors of the Monte's acting in the spirit of the founding bull and charged with reporting any negligence directly to the protector. Subsequently, on 2 May, it assigned a monthly salary equal to 25 *scudi* a year to the appraisers and remuneration of 40 *scudi* a year to the keeper of pledges.[84] We cannot be sure, however, whether these decisions broke new ground or merely put the stamp of approval on existing practice. The Monte's organisational structure gradually took shape, comprising two *provvisori* responsible for ordinary operations, a depositary or treasurer also tasked with keeping the accounts, one or more appraisers, one or more auditors and two guarantors. It appears that the auditors only checked the correctness of the statement of accounts, whereas the guarantors verified broad compliance with the institution's mission.

The first meetings of the congregation

Further adjustments were made on 8 May 1541, with two appraisers elected instead of the original one.[85] On 25 July the statement of accounts drawn up by the depositary Francesco Calciati was approved[86] and Calciati was replaced as accountant by Luigi Rucellai. Rucellai would later be appointed depositary, in 1543. The meeting of 25 July was the first known occasion on which the congregation approved what appear to have been the Monte's 'annual accounts'. None of its records survive to shed light on accounting procedures and results. In its first meeting of 1543 the congregation set the salary (30 *scudi*) and duties of the accountant.

On 27 July 1543 Angelo Massimo and Giovanni Antonio Zoni were elected *provvisori* and the term of office was lengthened to six months.[87] On 2 March 1544 the congregation increased the annual salary of the appraisers by 6 *scudi* and that of the keeper Agostino Pessina by 30.[88] It also clearly demarcated the latter's duties and authorised his wife being paid to assist him.

The first meetings of the congregation

The security of deposits of goods and cash was a recurring item on the agenda. On 14 May 1553, discussing the formal acceptance and custody of non-monetary deposits as well as cash, the congregation observed that such deposits had to be held by well-known, safe hands and decide to confer the responsibility upon the papal vicar for Rome, Filippo Archinto.

On 27 July 1546 the congregation formally approved the union of the Monte with the Ospedale di San Nicolò dei Boemi, although the formal contract had been concluded on 15 March 1546 with an act drawn up by the notary Cinziolino de' Galosio and witnessed by Agostino Pessina and Antonio de' Galosio.[89] This event brought down the curtain on the start-up period of the endeavour, which up to then more closely resembled a confraternity of patrons than a tightly-organised institution.

On 2 March 1547 the cashier Angelo Antonio Tasca died. His place was taken by Diego Algeziro, who remained in office at least until the late spring of 1560.[90]

On 14 October 1547 it was laid down that the congregation would be convened on the second Tuesday of each month at *'hora XX'*, but it is uncertain whether this applied only for those among its members who had been assigned operating tasks, i.e. a sort of board of directors.[91] It may be that the decision reflected the greater volume of work following the merger with the Ospedale.

The meeting of 20 March 1548 determined how cash loans to the indigent were to be organised (the text of the resolution describes some types of loan as 'alms') and decided that different rules and different locales should be used for making loans to indigent men and loans to women, subject to the approval and supervision of at least two delegates.[92] This decision may have been motivated not just by differences in creditworthiness between the sexes but also by the prevailing mores of the time.

On 10 July 1548 the congregation appointed two new cashier/keepers, the husband and wife Diego and Traquilla Algeziro, who had to post surety. Algeziro was already on the Monte's payroll as cashier, having taken over that position in the spring of 1547. The congregation also established the procedure for keeping the general accounts (those for which the depositary was responsible). These were to be entered in a book to be updated monthly and available for examination by the delegates.

The petty, daily and weekly accounts were kept by the cashier, who had to record the situation of cash on hand and give a

Table IX[95] *Payments and funds transfers for administrative activity of the Monte, 1540–74*

Date	Term	Amount	Counter-party
23 May 1540	short-term	sc. 50	depositor F. Calciati to cashier Tasca
29 May 1540	short-term	sc. 50	depositor F. Calciati to cashier Tasca
20 Sep. 1540	short-term	sc. 25	depositor F. Calciati to cashier Tasca
9 May 1541	short-term	sc. 50	depositor F. Calciati to cashier Tasca
9 May 1541	short-term	sc. 47 b. 20	cashier Tasca to depositor F. Calciati
9 Sep. 1574	short-term	sc. 500	Monte to depository of pledges[96]
Total		**sc. 722 b. 20**	

binding opinion of feasibility for each new pledge loan disbursement. Before entering into the service of the Monte, the cashier deposited surety for the correct performance of his official duties. By contrast, the depositaries did not make surety deposits, but in the first years at least they were called upon to make good the Monte's shortfalls out of their own pockets.[93] Table IX reports some financial transactions and payments made or authorised by the administration of the Monte beginning in 1540.

The accounting tasks of the depositary-accountant were apparently limited to general responsibility for drawing up the 'annual accounts' – as early as 1541 there is evidence of the congregation approving a sort of annual statement of accounts – and did not include the preparation of detailed accounts at fixed intervals. If the latter were prepared, it must have been at the discretion of the depositary. In any event, the developments described above seem more a miscellany of case-by-case improvements than a definitive rationalisation of the institution's organisational structure.

The effect of the merger with the Company of San Bernardo

Major change finally came on 13 August 1551, when representatives of the Monte and of the Company of San Bernardo agreed to merge the two institutions into a new Monte di Pietà of San Bernardo.[94] The first statutes of the Monte, issued on the occasion of the merger,[97] replaced the two *provvisori* with four 'guardian delegates', flanked by three delegates responsible for the accounts, a depository general, a cashier and two permanent secretaries having the function of attorneys. This organisational model, closely patterned on that of the Company of San Bernardo, lasted only until 1552. The reinstatement of the preceding model that year most likely signalled a reversal of the merger.

On 30 October 1551 the Monte's administrative structure was duly reorganised and officers were appointed to the newly created positions. The four guardians had a narrower mandate and less authority than the two *provvisori* whom they replaced. One of the guardians was a prelate, Bernardo de' Boni, who continued to act as the pope's personal referendary for the affairs of the Monte. It is probably fair to surmise that the role played by this representative and watchdog was connected with the merger and similar to that of the 'guarantors', instituted in 1541 but apparently not envisaged in the new organisational chart.

The functions of the accountant (keeping the books, preparing the 'financial statements' and inventories) were taken over by three delegates *pro indice*. For the first time since 1541, this position did not go to the same delegate who was appointed depositary. Alamanno degli Alamanni was designated depositary general and Donato Bonsignore cashier; Gian Giacomo Tassi and Alessandro Maroncelli were named secretaries with the special function of attorneys, the same position they had held in the Monte and the Company of San Bernardo respectively. The meeting of 30 October also appointed an assistant for the administration of pledged assets for each of the twelve districts of the historical centre of Rome.[98]

On 4 April 1552, however, the congregation decided to return to the pre-existing situation and restored the old functions and offices. A little later, on 30 May 1552, it considered a new arrangement: a plenary meeting to handle the business of the Monte and a 'select meeting' to appoint its officers, in part to obviate the problem of protracted vacancies due to the irregular intervals between meetings of the congregation. This too did not prove definitive, and the arrangement was modified by the Statutes of 1557. It was probably on that occasion that the administrative structure of the Monte began to stabilise, for it appears that the Borromean Statutes did not introduce sweeping changes.

Further modifications up to the Statutes of 1581

The changes introduced in the course of the succeeding years were largely incorporated in the official text of the Statutes of 1581, which remained in force without substantial amendment at least until 1617. In fact, Chapter III of the Statutes explicitly mentions the number and role of the principal officers and paid staff (*ministri*) of the Monte. The officers, elected annually by the Company, included three *provvisori* (one of whom was a prelate, an innovation dating from the early 1560s), two auditors (with functions comparable to those of the guarantors), four delegates with operating tasks, a secretary and thirteen councillors (one for each district of the city of Rome). The permanent, paid staff comprised the cashier, accountant, appraiser and custodian. These positions had changed very little over the years. By contrast, the administrative offices, held by members of the congregation, had been subject to repeated modification in terms of function, responsibility and number.

In the 1550s a project for a 'special committee' or 'executive committee' had been proposed for over a decade and was finally adopted in connection with the promulgation of the Statutes of 1557. On 5 August 1556 the congregation had approved the cardinal-protector's proposal for the creation of a sub-congregation formally entrusted with assisting the *provvisori* in the decisions regarding ordinary general business. Four members of the congregation – Alessandro Bartoli, Gian Pietro Cardelli, Bernardino del Conte and Gerolamo Guadagni – were named to this special committee, whose initial mandate was rather broad and concerned loan administration and auctions. Clearly, both the protector and the delegates were determined that the congregation should remain the supreme administrative organ. However, the special committee was also assigned the important task of preparing a draft of the official Statutes of the Monte for discussion and approval by the 'general congregation' (an expression that, in this context, signified an ordinary meeting of the delegates and should not be confused with the thrice-yearly meetings envisaged by the Statutes of 1581).

This first streamlined model of administration was subsequently modified. The Statutes of 1581 refer to bodies that are different in name but similar in function to the preceding ones: the ordinary congregation (annual), the general congregation (to be held three times a year) and the non-administrative annual meeting commemorating the deceased members of the confraternity.[100] In the event, the reshuffling of functions among the corporate bodies was often formal than substantive.

The issue of debate at the first meeting of the new committee, held on 16 August 1556 at the cloister of San Girolamo alla Regola, sheds light on the nature of the tasks the four delegates were to perform. Much of the discussion turned on the restructuring of the Monte's creditor positions, which included a high incidence of bad debts. The committee decided to renegotiate all the defaulted loans, without detriment to the amount due to the custodian of pledges Agostino Pessina, to estimate the hypothetical losses arising from the sale of the related collateral and thus to estimate the realisable value of those pledged assets. The committee also examined the first official draft of the new Statutes, deciding to submit it to the next general meeting for final approval. That meeting took place on 29 March 1557 and formally adopted the Monte's first true Statutes.[101]

The new four-man committee met for the first time on 3 April 1557 in the presence of the *provvisori* in the convent attached to the Church of San Salvatore in Lauro.

The following years saw the congregation adopt further measures to improve administrative control and organisational efficiency. On 2 January 1559 it appointed a delegate to audit the records of goods pledged in 1555–56, evidence that the quality of management of the warehouse and depository still left a good deal to be desired. In 1560 it decided that if a pledged asset was not sufficient to cover the value of the loan, the officer who had accepted it would be held personally responsible.[102] On 11 July 1563 it provided for a list of items sold to be compiled every month, a decision confirmed in subsequent resolutions. Thus, on 2 August 1563 the congregation ordered that an inventory be taken of assets to be sold, that these be assembled before the auction in the exhibition room, and that a copy of the list of items be handed to the delegate supervising the auction.[103] Returning to the question on 24 February 1571, it ordered an audit of goods and cash to be conducted yearly, with the financial statements to be prepared for approval by a general congregation.[104]

For the Monte's further protection, it was decided on 15 February 1568 that the custodian was not allowed to receive pledged assets or pawn tickets nor to release an asset except in the presence of the appointed delegates, under pain of loss of office and a fine of 25 *scudi*.[105] This partly ran counter to a resolution of 25 October 1564 authorising easily salable items of little value to be released to junk dealers for subsequent sale. But practice often enough strayed from formal guidelines. On 24 January 1584, for example, we find the accountant, one Pietro Paolo, being directed to 'make his writing understood' or else pay for an audit, i.e. make good any shortfall.[106]

The development of the Monte's administrative structure in its early years reflects an ongoing attempt to cope with growth. The efficiency it achieved over time points to its expanding role within the papal administration. Proof of this is to be found in the Statutes of 1581, which summed up the efforts of successive administrations and created a formal framework of rules for future action.

Rigorous respect for orthodoxy and a determination to play an important role in an 'institutional' capacity are fully evident in the preamble to the Statutes:

> ...With the intent of establishing in this fair City a Monte di Pietà, but knowing that this most holy endeavour would not be likely to make progress without the authority and approbation of the Holy Apostolic See, and having beseeched the Holy Memory of [Paul III] and that of Pius IV, a grant was made, as is shown by their bulls recorded below, of permission to establish the Monte, with the institution of a Company benefiting from many privileges, indulgences and kindnesses, and of the authority to make statutes for the good government of the Monte, with the right to add and subtract in the future, as demanded by the changing times...[107]

The salaries of the Monte's permanent employees

Salary payments between 1541 and 1562

In its early years the Monte had a 'permanent' staff of between three and five employees. Tome 39 of the *Registri dei Decreti di congregazione (1540–1566)* contains a long section of entries concerning the monthly payments by the cashier to employees. These entries, drawn up by the accountant and secretary, Gian Giacomo Tassi, follow a very simple formula, i.e.:

> By order of the Provvisori of the Sacro Monte della Pietà di Roma, you, Messer Angelo Antonio Tasca, cashier of said Monte, are directed to pay to the three salaried officers of said Monte for their compensation for the month of [...] 9 and one-half *scudi* and to obtain their receipt and to enter the figure in the account of said Monte.

In the years 1541 and 1542 the 'salaried officers' were three: the secretary, the appraiser and the custodian. The latter came to

Salary payments between 1541 and 1562

be permanently assisted by his wife, who was granted a status similar to her husband's.

These entries are the first available. Although the Monte may have hired permanent employees only in the second year of the protectorate of Cardinal Rodolfo Pio di Carpi, this leaves unanswered the question of the earlier status of the cashier, appraiser and custodian. Possibly, the salaries were not paid directly by the Monte but were included in the expenses defrayed by the founders, but this seems rather far-fetched, since no trace of such an arrangement is to be found in the minutes of the congregation. More plausibly, the functions were 'outsourced' to merchants who were members of the congregation. The salaries paid by the Monte in 1541 are shown in Table X.[108]

In the first years the Monte's cashier earned 4 *scudi* a month, the accountant 2, the appraiser just over 2 (25 *scudi* a year) and the custodian around 3½ (40 *scudi* a year). The congregation set the salaries of the appraiser and the accountant on 2 May 1541 and that of the accountant on 10 January 1543. The annual payroll rose from around 114 *scudi* in 1542 to 154 *scudi* in 1543 and averaged 180 in the subsequent years.

Salaries were not paid on a fixed day, although pay day usually fell at the end of the month or early in the subsequent month. The payroll grew from 9½ *scudi* for three employees to 12½ for four and 15 *scudi* for a staff of five when the custodian's wife was granted employee status in February 1544. She drew 2½ *scudi*, one less than her husband; since there is an entry noting that each 'salaried officer' received 3 *scudi* a month, the difference doubtless reflects averaging between the two.

The number of salaried employees on the Monte's payroll grew to four in January 1543 and five in March 1544. The salary payments for the years from 1545 onwards are shown in Tables XIV–XX.

Payments changed to every two months from 1547. The change may have been made with a view to rationalising cash flows or could have been connected with the death of the cashier, Angelo Antonio Tasca, who by 2 March of that year had been replaced by Diego Algeziro.

Although the total payroll remained unchanged between the Jubilee Year of 1550 and 1552, the Monte decided on a salary equalisation at 3 *scudi* a month, paid every two months.[109] This may have been prompted by the merger with the Company of San Bernardo; in the event, the subsequent reversal of that union brought pay levelling to a halt until 1555. Beginning that year,

Table x   *Salaries paid, 1541*

Date	Month	Payment	Payees
1 July 1541	June	sc. 9½	cashier, appraiser, custodian
2 Aug. 1541	July	sc. 9½	cashier, appraiser, custodian
5 Sep. 1541	Aug.	sc. 9½	cashier, appraiser, custodian
7 Oct. 1541	Sep.	sc. 9½	cashier, appraiser, custodian
20 Oct. 1541	Oct.	sc. 9½	cashier, appraiser, custodian
Nov. 1541	Nov.	sc. 9½	cashier, appraiser, custodian
23 Dec. 1541	Dec.	sc. 9½	cashier, appraiser, custodian
Total 1541	7 months	**sc. 66½**	3 employees

Table xi   *Salaries paid, 1542*

Date	Month	Payment	Payees
3 Feb. 1542	Jan.	sc. 9½	cashier, appraiser, custodian
23 Feb. 1542	Feb.	sc. 9½	cashier, appraiser, custodian
9 Mar. 1542	Mar.	sc. 9½	cashier, appraiser, custodian
1 June 1542	Apr.	sc. 9½	cashier, appraiser, custodian
30 June 1542	May	sc. 9½	cashier, appraiser, custodian
28 July 1542	June	sc. 9½	cashier, appraiser, custodian
Aug. 1542	July	sc. 9½	cashier, appraiser, custodian
2 Sep. 1542	Aug.	sc. 9½	cashier, appraiser, custodian
2 Oct. 1542	Sep.	sc. 9½	cashier, appraiser, custodian
28 Oct. 1542	Oct.	sc. 9½	cashier, appraiser, custodian
4 Dec. 1542	Nov.	sc. 9½	cashier, appraiser, custodian
28 Dec. 1542	Dec.	sc. 9½	cashier, appraiser, custodian
Total 1542	12 months	**sc. 114**	3 employees

each employee received 6 *scudi* every two months, regardless of seniority. No provision was made for year-end bonuses or the like.

From July 1560 onwards the payments were no longer made by the cashier but directly by the depositary. One reason why the series of accounting records ends in early 1562 may have been that the depositary, usually a banker, wrote the entries directly to the Monte's account with his own bank, an arrangement similar to that used by the Apostolic Chamber. If so, the Monte must have kept a mirror copy of the depositary's entries, so that both parties could periodically cross-check and endorse each other's account book. No trace of such accounts survives, however. The entry of 1 July 1560 mentions new monthly salaries: 4 *scudi* for

Salary payments between 1541 and 1562

Table XII *Salaries paid, 1543*

Date	Month	Payment	Payees
5 Feb. 1543	Jan.	sc. 12½	cashier, appraiser, custodian, accountant
2 Mar. 1543	Feb.	sc. 12½	as above
30 Mar. 1543	Mar.	sc. 12½	as above
25 Apr. 1543	Apr.	sc. 12½	as above
1 June 1543	May	sc. 12½	as above
2 July 1543	June	sc. 12½	as above
30 July 1543	July	sc. 12½	as above
1 Sep. 1543	Aug.	sc. 12½	as above
1 Oct. 1543	Sep.	sc. 12½	as above
2 Nov. 1543	Oct.	sc. 12½	as above
30 Nov. 1543	Nov.	sc. 12½ + 2	cashier, appraiser, 2 custodians, accountant
31 Dec. 1543	Dec.	sc. 12½ + 2	as above
Total 1543	12 months	**sc. 154**	4 employees and custodian's wife[111]

Camillo, the custodian, 3 for Diego Algeziro, the cashier, 2 for Giovanni, the accountant, and 3 for Agostino Pessina, the appraiser.

The era of uniform pay had been short. The return to a pay scale may have been a recognition of the need to reward different skills and duties differently, not least as an inducement to the custodian to stem the chronic losses at the depository. It is interesting that the records continue to refer to five employees, indicating that, as in the past, the custodians were a couple. On 22 May Giovanni Servilio was appointed as the new accountant with a monthly salary of 2 *scudi*. Servilio took office on 5 June.

Although the series of payment entries breaks off in 1562, some further information on salaries is available. On 13 August 1565 the congregation set a ceiling of 2 *scudi* on the monthly salaries of the attorneys, cashier and custodian, well below the past peaks of between 4 and 5 *scudi*. This made it clear to the staff that their positions were not sinecures; authentic dedication to the institution's mission may have made it easier to accept little more than a servant was paid. Then, on 10 September 1565, for the first time in the history of the Monte, the congregation directed the *provvisori* to fine some absentees.[110]

Banking and Charity in Sixteenth-Century Italy

Table XIII *Salaries paid, 1544*

Date	Month	Payment	Payees
8 Feb. 1544	Jan.	sc. 12½ + 2	cashier, appraiser, 2 custodians, accountant
28 Feb. 1544	Feb.	sc. 12½ + 2	as above
4 Apr. 1544	Mar.	sc. 15	as above
5 May 1544	Apr.	sc. 15	as above
6 June 1544	May	sc. 15	as above
4 July 1544	June	sc. 15	as above
31 July 1544	July	sc. 15	as above
1 Sep. 1544	Aug.	sc. 15	as above
3 Oct. 1544	Sep.	sc. 15	as above
31 Oct. 1544	Oct.	sc. 15	as above
5 Dec. 1544	Nov.	sc. 15	as above
19 Dec. 1544	Dec.	sc. 15	as above
Total 1544	12 months	**sc. 179**	5 employees

Table XIV *Salaries paid, 1545*

Date	Month	Payment	Payees
3 Feb. 1545	Jan.	sc. 15	cashier, appraiser, 2 custodians, accountant
2 Mar. 1545	Feb.	sc. 15	as above
31 Mar. 1545	Mar.	sc. 15	as above
4 May 1545	Apr.	sc. 15	as above
5 June 1545	May	sc. 15	as above
7 July 1545	June	sc. 15	as above
31 July 1545	July	sc. 15	as above
1 Sep. 1545	Aug.	sc. 15	as above
2 Oct. 1545	Sep.	sc. 15	as above
6 Nov. 1545	Oct.	sc. 15	as above
4 Dec. 1545	Nov.	sc. 15	as above
31 Dec. 1545	Dec.	sc. 15	as above
Total 1545	12 months	**sc. 180**	5 employees

This approach must have met with resistance, or perhaps it dawned on the management that a decent wage was the best guarantee of diligence, for on 13 August 1566 the congregation authorised salaries of 7 *scudi* a month for the custodian and 4 *scudi* for the cashier, and voted to pay the appraiser 2 *baiocchi* per *scudo*

Salary payments between 1541 and 1562

Table XV *Salaries paid, 1546*

Date	Month	Payment	Payees
31 Jan. 1546	Jan.	sc. 15	cashier, appraiser, 2 custodians, accountant
1 Mar. 1546	Feb.	sc. 15	as above
2 Apr. 1546	Mar.	sc. 15	as above
30 Apr. 1546	Apr.	sc. 15	as above
1 June 1546	May	sc. 15	as above
1 July 1546	June	sc. 15	as above
6 Aug. 1546	July	sc. 15	as above
3 Sep. 1546	Aug.	sc. 15	as above
1 Oct. 1546	Sep.	sc. 15	as above
5 Nov. 1546	Oct.	sc. 15	as above
3 Dec. 1546	Nov.	sc. 15	as above
31 Dec. 1546	Dec.	sc. 15	as above
Total 1546	12 months	**sc. 180**	5 employees

Table XVI *Salaries paid, 1547*

Date	Month	Payment	Payees
28 Feb. 1547	Jan./Feb.	sc. 30	cashier, appraiser, 2 custodians, accountant
6 May 1547	Mar./Apr.	sc. 30	as above
23 June 1547	May/June	sc. 30	as above
2 Sep. 1547	July/Aug.	sc. 30	as above
4 Nov. 1547	Sep./Oct.	sc. 30	as above
23 Dec. 1547	Nov./Dec.	sc. 30	as above
Total 1547	12 months	**sc. 180**	5 employees

Table XVII *Salaries paid, 1559*

Date	Month	Payment	Payees
6 Mar. 1559	Jan./Feb.	sc. 30	cashier, appraiser, 2 custodians, accountant
1 May 1559	Mar./Apr.	sc. 30	as above
1 July 1559	May/June	sc. 29	as above
4 Sep. 1559	July/Aug.	sc. 28	as above
3 Nov. 1559	Sep./Oct.	sc. 28	as above
2 Jan. 1560	Nov./Dec.	sc. 28	as above
Total 1559	12 months	**sc. 173**	5 employees

Banking and Charity in Sixteenth-Century Italy

Table XVIII *Salaries paid, 1560*

Date	Month	Payment	Payees
1 Mar. 1560	Jan./Feb.	sc. 28	cashier, appraiser, 2 custodians, accountant
2 May 1560	Mar./Apr.	sc. 24	as above
1 July 1560	May/June	sc. 24	as above
2 Sep. 1560	July/Aug.	sc. 20	as above
28 Oct. 1560	Sep./Oct.	sc. 20	as above
2 Jan. 1561	Nov./Dec.	sc. 20	as above
Total 1560	12 months	**sc. 136**	5 employees

Table XIX *Salaries paid, 1561*

Date	Month	Payment	Payees
27 Feb. 1561	Jan./Feb.	sc. 20	cashier, appraiser, 2 custodians, accountant
no date	Mar./Apr.	sc. 20	as above
4 July 1561	May/June	sc. 20	as above
1 Sep. 1561	July/Aug.	sc. 20	as above
24 Nov. 1561	Sep./Oct.	sc. 20	as above
29 Dec. 1561	Nov./Dec.	sc. 20	as above
Total 1561	12 months	**sc. 120**	5 employees

Table XX *Salaries paid, 1562*

Date	Month	Payment	Payees
1 Apr. 1562	Jan./Feb.	sc. 20	cashier, appraiser, 2 custodians, accountant
4 May 1562	Mar./Apr.	sc. 20	as above
Total 1562	4 months	**sc. 40**	5 employees

on the proceeds from auctions.[112] This softer line continued with the meeting of 20 May 1572, which accompanied an increase of 1 *scudo* in the accountant's salary with the recommendation to keep the books up to date. Shortly thereafter, on 28 June, the congregation, considering that the custodian had 'an assistant', raised his monthly salary by 3 *scudi*.[113]

On 28 July 1573 the annual salary of the cashier was raised by 5 *scudi* and 50 *baiocchi*, the custodian's by 12 *scudi*, the accountant's by 5 *scudi* and 50 *baiocchi* and the appraiser's by 2 *scudi* and 50 *baiocchi*. On 4 May 1574 Rutilio Strozzi was appointed accountant with a salary of 2 *scudi* a month, but with the commitment to make over half of this amount to pay off a debt he had with his father. On 2 June 1574 the custodians' pay was raised. On 6 July 1574 a new custodian was appointed, and on 13 July of that year Girolamo Galli was named custodian with a salary of 13 *scudi* a month. On the last day of February 1577 Girolamo Adelato was appointed cashier with a salary of 5 gold *scudi*. On 3 September 1577 the attorney's pay was reduced to 1 *scudo* a month 'on account of slack business'.[114] On 21 May 1578 it was decided that a delegate could stand in for an absent *provvisore*. These decisions generally bring to mind personnel management issues that crop up in modern firms. In this respect, at least, the situation at the Monte appears to have been not altogether unlike latter models of employee–employer relations.

A case of public intervention in the economy

The Monte di Pietà of Rome as an economic agency

If the creation of the Monte di Pietà of Rome reflected Franciscan ideals of applying Christian ethics and solidarity to the field of credit, by the end of the sixteenth century the Monte, in vastly different circumstances, had been brought into the orbit of the papal administration. Factors ranging from the plague of 1576 to the repercussions of the inflow of gold and silver from the New World to Spain's repeated economic and financial woes conspired to worsen general economic conditions. The first half of the seventeenth century would be recorded as one of the most difficult periods in European economic history.[115] In Italy's maritime cities and other commercial centres, as the rate of return fell, capital was withdrawn from commerce and industry and invested in finance and land.[116] The reverberations of the international situation were palpable in Rome, where the Monte di Pietà made some 25,000 or 26,000 pledge loans a year to a population of between 50,000 and 70,000, of whom more than 20,000 worked in craft production.[117] In fact, assisting the weakest strata of society was the principal function the Monte performed on behalf of the state in the late sixteenth century.

The Monte of Rome was not unique in being absorbed into the public administration. Indeed, that of Naples, its exact contemporary, entered the public orbit much earlier and faster, by government decree. As Luigi De Rosa recounts,

Around the 1570s the viceregal government recognised the *fedi di credito* of the Monte di Pietà of Naples, which could be made over by endorsement, to be valid as full discharge in payments of amounts due to the state. This was of appreciable help to the activity of the Monte, which not only began to raise funds from public entities as well as from private individuals but also saw its *fedi di credito* enjoy ever-increasing favour.[118]

The Monte's slow evolution into a state bank

By and large, the transformation of *monti di pietà* into banks in every respect was a slow process extending into the late eighteenth and early nineteenth centuries or even later,[119] and when it did occur it was merely the final step of a seemingly natural course of events, an act whereby the authorities or the institutions' governing bodies acknowledged reality and fitted form to fact. The Monte of Rome constitutes a notable exception. Although a relative latecomer, it took the initiative of acting as a bank before the end of the sixteenth century, even before the conferral in October 1584 of the Deposit Bank for Judicial Proceedings, and from then on increasingly performed the role of 'state bank'. This role was reinforced by the appointment of the Monte in 1743 to run the papal treasury as depositary of the Apostolic Chamber, a position hitherto reserved to private bankers, and was fully formalised during the next century when the Monte took over the activities of state mint and became the central bank in all but name. The strategic importance of the institution probably played a part in this transformation, which unfolded under the stringent control and direction of the governmental authorities. As the Monte developed into an arm of the state, the role of the merchant bankers who had supported it early on, participating directly in its administration or financing it in those times of chronic cash shortages, came to an end.

It should also be recalled that the pre-eminence attributed to the Monte di Pietà of Rome as first among equals implied an increasing integration of its functions with those of the papal government. This was partly dictated by reasons of prestige, but it also probably reflected an assessment of the Monte as a flexible and appropriate instrument with which to respond to genuine social needs, considering the range of services it supplied even before the end of the sixteenth century.[120]

As mentioned, on 20 March 1548 the *congregazione* resolved to petition the pope for a general privilege facilitating not only bequests in favour of the Monte but also the use of customer deposits.[121] While the former may not have been a novel request,

The Monte's slow evolution into a state bank

the latter certainly was. Specifically, the board requested that the Monte be authorised to transfer the funds it raised, albeit still without apparently granting any remuneration to depositors, and that the board itself be allowed to extend these benefits and other indulgences to affiliated Monti outside of Rome (*'extra urbe'*). Transferability of deposits, requested at a time when the Monte still did not demand any remuneration of loans (the resolution on the 'reimbursement of expenses' dates from 1552), involved far more than an administrative convenience, for it made it possible for the Monte to transfer idle funds to other (mainly private) banks through exchange transactions paying a 'market rate', thus giving it some return on capital without breaking any of its fundamental rules.

By authorising the Monte to carry out transactions that had been typical of private banks, the privilege bestowed an effective banking function on it for the first time. But beyond this timid attempt to enter the arena of competition in the credit market through the back door, the board's proposal implied turning the Monte of Rome into a central credit institution for other *monti*, not only confirming its primacy but enabling its board to exercise explicit authority.[122]

The Monte's recurring financial crises in its early years probably bulked large in the papal authorities' decisions to support the institution with measures that turned it essentially into a bank, without detriment to its original social welfare and charitable purposes. The events examined here represented the first step in the transformation of the Monte from a simple creation of a confraternity of benefactors (the 'Company') into a banking institution that eventually performed the functions of central bank of the papal state. Among other milestones before the conferral of the Deposit Bank were the 1552 resolution on reimbursement of expenses,[123] numerous resolutions laying down the rules and procedures for fund-raising, the summary records of which explicitly mention 'interest' as the premium paid to depositors,[124] and the forging of an efficient administrative and operating structure.

The resolutions of 20 March 1548 paved the way for transferable debt securities, the *luoghi* that the Monte began to issue in the early 1570s and that gave it an efficient method of funding. As the Monte increasingly assumed a public function typical of a state entity, these securities assumed the characteristics of sovereign debt and eventually became one of the forms of the public debt.

59

Whether this debt was actually turned into productive capital, as was often the case with the public debt funds of the administration of Rome, or served only to support the poor and needy is not entirely clear.[125] While the Monte's credit function was oriented more to consumption than to investment, in the course of the sixteenth century the institution became a pre-eminent place of encounter between those with capital to spare and the needs of the lower classes, from the indigent and unemployed to wage workers and even small artisans and shopkeepers, especially in times of crisis. The question is how far did the Monte's credit serve a purely welfare function, financing basic consumption to the exclusion of petty production. The available data do not support a definitive answer, but they do indicate that the Monte was a driving force in the Roman economy; the very popularity of borrowing from the Monte, as evidenced by the number of loans granted per year, suggest that its role went well beyond supplying consumption credit to the needy.

In the early seventeenth century the Monti terminated the practice of requesting modest reimbursement for expenses on pledge loans and reverted to lending entirely free of charge.[126] This marked the passage from the Monte's original charitable and welfare function to the considerably more important one of disbursing aid and subsidies to the local economy.[127] However, given the Monte's status as an institution protected by law, all this ultimately heralded the substantial destruction of the local credit market, up to then dominated by Jewish moneylenders. The Monte, then, was not an unalloyed blessing for the community: its social merits must be weighed against the setback the local economy suffered as a result of the blow dealt to Rome's small banks. Indeed, such an attempt to orient and direct the economy may inherently involve a negation of the 'credit market' in its modern form.[128]

The conferral of the Bank of Deposits for Judicial Proceedings was consistent with a long-standing trend. Enjoying de facto status akin to that of a governmental entity practically from its inception, the Monte had increasingly taken on the traits and tasks of a public banking institution. This reading of the logic of the chain of events seems sounder than the reductive view that the Monte was simply the object of a bail-out, that it was rescued from certain bankruptcy only for reasons of prestige and to avoid repudiating the rather widespread model it represented. All this happened with the implicit blessing of the papal authorities, who ensured the institution's solidity and function and endorsed its status as an effective part of the public administration even before historical circumstances led to its actual inclusion in the state sphere.

Ultimately, it matters little that this singular process of public intervention in the economy originated in the question of usury and in the disputes on interest. A pointer in this direction is offered by Keynes in the Appendix to the General Theory, where he remarks:

> I was brought up to believe that the attitude of the Medieval Church to the rate of interest was inherently absurd, and that the subtle discussions aimed at distinguishing the return on money loans from the return to active investment were merely Jesuitical attempts to find a practical escape from a foolish theory. But I now read these discussions as an honest intellectual effort to keep separate what the classical theory has inextricably confused together, namely the rate of interest and the marginal efficiency of capital.[129]

Pursuing this line of reasoning, in retrospect the *monti di pietà* can be viewed as an instrument of economic policy and not merely as an expedient designed to circumvent rules that could only be applied at the risk of harming the economy as a whole. Again, following Keynes and his emphasis on the pre-eminence of public economic intervention during cyclical downturns, and taking care not to stretch the point, several aspects of the *monti* experience deserve consideration: the attempt to bring the small loan market 'under control', the desire to use the *monti di pietà* for social purposes, the determination to centralise important economic decisions and limit the weight of what today would be called the free market.

Is such an approach to the problem plausible? It is historically correct? How much weight did the claims of faith effectively carry against those of economic necessity? It could be argued that the extreme position of doing away with interest (or 'reimbursement of expenses') on loans was actually designed to eliminate any and every form of credit market, a goal that was partly achieved with the fading away of the local moneylenders. On the other hand, measured against the rise of the Atlantic economies and the Protestant Reformation, changes in local policies contributed little to the eclipse of the great Italian international merchant bankers (with the exception of the Genoese for a spell at the end of the sixteenth century). Possibly, the decay of banking undercut manufacturing or at least catalysed a change in the structure of the economy and society, but this again was due to factors that lay beyond Rome and were at work in most of Europe. Insofar as local policy shaped economic conditions in Rome, it ushered in a period in which local activity was held broadly 'stationary' in the Schumpeterian sense[130] and bound by central directives. On the other hand, the spiritual motivation behind these directives precluded ambitions even remotely resembling those that in recent times have inspired state socialism.

In the end it must be admitted that the sources are too sketchy to permit more than interesting speculation on these questions, but they leave no doubt as to the importance of the public role that the Monte di Pietà of Rome played in the local economy from the late sixteenth century onwards.

Notes

1   ASMP, '*Nota Decretorum Congregationis 1540–1604*', references to 1565.
2   For this and the subsequent resolutions of the congregation, see ASMP, '*Nota Decretorum Congregationis 1540–1604*', references to 1578–82.
3   See M. Fornasari, *Il Tesoro della città*, pp.44 ff. for the Monte di Pietà of Bologna between July 1473 and December 1474. According to. Fornasari, its activity consisted mainly in pawnbroking. The only deposits taken during the first few months were advances from members of the company or outright donations.
4   M. Tosi, *op. cit.*, p.41, reports that interest was paid on deposits and bequests before 1552. For some later cases, see Table III.
5   The resolution in question is in ASMP, Tome 13, '*Registri di Brevi, Instromenti e Decreti di Congregazione, 1540–1604*', section relative to the '*Nota Decretorum Congregationis 1540–1604*', references to 1569. On 23 March 1579 the Protector, Francesco Alciati, issued a notice that deposits would thenceforth bear no interest. On 7 February 1584 the congregation decided that interest should no longer be paid on deposits, but it is not clear whether this was intended as a general rule for the future or represented a unilateral moratorium due to a temporary shortage of funds. The resolution directed anyone demanding the interest payable to him to appeal to the pope. It is not known if this resolution was ever implemented. *Ibid.*, references to 1579 and 1584.
6   ASMP, Tome 13, '*Registri di Brevi, Instromenti e Decreti di Congregazione, 1540–1604*', section relative to the '*Nota Decretorum Congregationis 1540–1604*', references to 1569.
7   Giovanni Rucellai, Gian Pietro Crivelli and Francesco Calciati were among the bankers (and in some cases patrons) who dealt with the Monte from its foundation.
8   The earliest surviving document confirming the transferability of deposits is a resolution dated 2 April 1565 whereby the congregation decided that an annuity of 18 *scudi* made out to one Flavio Cesalino should be turned over to Carlo de' Crescenzi. This was the first formal authorisation for the transfer of a legacy – annuities were generally paid out of tied deposits – to a third party.
9   Travellers commonly arranged for a banker to transmit funds to their destination, in order avoid carrying all the money they needed with them. This business was monopolised by the great international firms with branches or partners in all the leading financial centres. See R. de Roover, *The Rise and Decline of the Medici Bank, op. cit.*, chapters I, II and VIII, and J. Favier, *op. cit.*, pp.72 ff.
10 The main difference between *cedole* and *luoghi* was the relative liquidity of the latter. A *luogo* resembled a security, whereas a *cedola* was essentially a certificate of deposit that only the depositor could redeem at the Monte's offices. On the other hand, whereas *luoghi* were payable forward, *cedole* essentially represented short-term liabilities, since they simply attested to a transacted deposit, and were therefore the more flexible instrument. On *cedole*, see C.M. Travaglini, *op. cit.*, pp.471–85. The first evidence of the issue of *luoghi* dates from the early 1570s. See ASMP, Tome 13, '*Registri di Brevi,*

Notes to Chapter II

Instromenti e Decreti di Congregazione, 1540–1604', section relative to the '*Nota Decretorum Congregationis 1540–1604*', references to 1571 and subsequent years.

11 Traces of non-interest bearing deposits are to be found in the second part of Tome 39, '*Registri dei Decreti di Congregazione, 1540–1566*'. The word 'copy' is written next to each entry.

12 See D. Tamilia, *op. cit.*, chapter I. Tosi is of the same opinion, adding that the early depositors included many notables, Giulia Colonna for one. M. Tosi, *op. cit.*, p.39.

13 ASMP, '*Registro di Lettere Apostoliche ed Instromenti Diversi*', c.71.

14 A similar comparison can be made for Bologna, where holders of *luoghi* were paid interest of between 4 and 10 per cent, depending on whether the securities they held were unredeemable or fixed-term. See M. Carboni, *Il debito della città – Mercato del credito, fisco e società a Bologna fra Cinque e seicento*, Bologna, Il Mulino, 1995, pp.78–82.

15 Source: based on F. Colzi, *op. cit.*, Table III.a, p.146. The figures refer to the aggregate public debt of Rome in the form of *luoghi* and other debt securities issued by government expenditure funds. These instruments were quite widely held and 'liquid', as they were transferable, and can therefore be used as a benchmark for the market cost of debt in Rome in the mid-1500s.

16 These were almost always backed by tax revenues or rents; technically, they paid holders not interest but a share in the 'yield' of these sources.

17 The sources indicate that the Monte contracted this obligation in order to repay another liability.

18 Source: notations in '*Registri dei Decreti di Congregazione 1540–1566*' (Tome 39) o '*Nota Decretorum Congregationis 1540–1604*'.

19 A deposit for a case pending. The amount was to be repaid by the Monte in monthly instalments of 100 *scudi*, but on 25 June 1562 Orsini's administrator, Riccardo Mazatosto, assigned the remaining claim of 806 *scudi* to Fra Giulio Sordo of San Miniato and instructed the Monte to make immediate payment, which it promptly did.

20 Refers to residual back payments of rent on several buildings plus arrears of interest.

21 The duration of this deposit is unknown; despite appearances, it surely did not bear 50 per cent interest.

22 The resolution of 27 January 1561 approved borrowing 800 *scudi* at 8 per cent a year. That of 4 October 1563 approved raising 900 *scudi* but did not explicitly mention interest rates or duration. On 17 September 1565 the congregation decided that the Monte would pay 6 per cent on borrowings of up to 500 *scudi*, 8 per cent on amounts of between 500 and 1,000 *scudi* and 9 per cent on larger amounts, including legacies. ASMP, '*Nota Decretorum Congregationis 1540–1604*', references to 1561–5.

23 ASMP, *Raccolta di Bolle e Privilegi del Sacro Monte della Pietà di Roma*, c.31.

24 On 5 December 1581 the congregation ordered that an inventory be taken of the goods held in pledge, with the records to be drawn up by 3 April 1582. ASMP, '*Registri di Brevi, Instromenti e Decreti di Congregazione, 1540–1604*', Tome 13, the part relative to the '*Nota Decretorum Congregationis 1540–1604*', references to 1581 and 1582. A brief issued by Pope Pius IV on 21 August 1560 made the cardinal-protector of the Monte di Pietà of Rome a judge for all the legal actions and questions to which the Monte was a party, foreshadowing the fuller governmental role of the Monte.

25 ASR, annex in Via Gallia Placidia, *Libro mastro di contro del Banco dei Depositi del Sacro Monte di Pietà di Roma, anno 1585*, c.1.

26 As noted earlier, it is plausible that *cedole* (hence deposits) were an effective instrument of funding from the very inception. Specific accounting records showing the link between deposits and loans are lacking, however.

27 ASR, *Libro mastro 1585*, cc.3–75, summary accounts.

28 F. Colzi, *op. cit.*, pp.88 ff., observes that the so-called old Monte della Carne, whose first issue dated from 1556, was the second public debt fund established by the municipal administration of Rome (the first was the Monte della Farina, established in 1552). Debt was issued in 1556 in order to pay for defensive works for Rome against the expected attack by the Spanish troops under the Duke of Alba. A 30-year tax was imposed on meat as backing for the issue. The peace of 12 September 1557 averted a second sack of Rome. Instead of expiring, the Monte della Carne and the related meat tax were extended repeatedly and became permanent. The Monte della Carne was finally extinguished in 1573. A second Monte della Carne was established in 1576 and lasted until 1660.

29 For the first decade of activity, see Table I. It is reasonable to suppose that this estimate also holds for the subsequent decades, since staff costs remained virtually unchanged and there was no reason for further rises in other expenses, except for possible loan losses on a growing loan portfolio. On the same assumption adopted in Table I, with loan estimates estimated at 5 per cent of annual loans up to 1560, the estimate for the first ten years of activity remains fully valid.

30 Source: ASMP, entries in *'Registri dei Decreti di Congregazione, 1540–1566'*, Tome 39, or *'Nota Decretorum Congregationis 1540–1604'*.

31 Dowry offered with a promise of 2 October 1553 by the bishop of Malta to Maddalena, daughter of the saddler Zanobio, to be paid after verification of the wedding.

32 Instalment of payment for legal acts for the merger with the Ospedale dei Boemi. This was also the reason for the payment of 18 *scudi* to the same notary on 4 July 1561.

33 Rent for buildings used by the Monte.

34 Restoration of houses of the Monte at Santa Lucia alla Chiavica.

35 The payment was made to the Abbess of San Silvestro for Isabella, daughter of Cesare Papi.

36 The funding requirement of 3000 *scudi* a year is an estimate based on the assumptions adopted in Table VIII. It is derived by calculating the total financial commitment as equal to around 60 per cent of the total amount of capital lent each year, taking into account the practice of making loans for terms of six months, gaps between loans and non-performing loans.

37 This equivalence holds for other *monti di pietà* as well. The debt securities of that of Naples, for example, were officially declared to be fungible with government securities from the 1570s onwards. See L. De Rosa, 'Storia della Banca e della Borsa', in *Dizionario di Banca, Borsa e Finanza*, Rome, Ipsoa, 1993, vol. I, p.18.

38 On the public debt, see F. Colzi, *op. cit.*, pp.65–178; also, F. Piola Caselli, 'La diffusione dei luoghi di monte della Camera Apostolica alla fine del XVI secolo', in *Atti del primo Convegno Nazionale (4–6 giugno 1987) della Società Italiana degli storici dell'economia su 'Credito e sviluppo economico in Italia dal Medioevo all'Età Contemporanea'*, Verona, 1988.

39 According to Fornasari, in Bologna the *monte* followed a similar practice. Its depositors included 'two "governors" – the depositary and the book-keeper – who at a time of heavy demand for credit, in July 1473, deposited a sizable sum of money, which shows that the initiative was entrusted to the good will and charity of these "special individuals" '. M. Fornasari, *op. cit.*, p.48. The books of the Monte di Pietà of Rome show large surety deposits by the depositary Luigi Rucellai and Angelo Massimo (see Table III).

40 On 23 June 1573 the Monte decided to accept a legacy of 152 *scudi* for an annuity of 7½ *scudi* payable to Tiberio de Marsianis (act drawn up by Fermo Calvi, apostolic notary). On 20 September 1575 it accepted a testamentary legacy of 200 *scudi* in *luoghi* of the Monte left by Andrea Pelato. On 5 July 1582 it accepted a legacy of 150 *scudi* from an unnamed pilgrim (the document drawn up by Francesco Pechinali, notary, is mentioned). ASMP, Tome 13, *'Registri di Brevi, Instromenti e Decreti di Congregazione, 1540–1604'*, section relative to the *'Nota Decretorum Congregationis 1540–1604'*, references to 1573, 1575 and 1582.

41 Source: based on F. Colzi, *op cit.*, Table III.a., p.146. Debt securities comprises *luoghi* and other securities issued by public debt funds of the administration of Rome.

42 In Bologna, the local *monte* 'derived part of its financial resources from deposits, most of them voluntary, but it might be better to call them loans, from a small group of citizens who … entrusted their money to the Monte for it to use for a definite period of time or else for "as long as our Monte lasts"'. M. Fornasari, *op. cit.*, p.47.

43 ASMP, Tome 13, *'Registri di Brevi, Instromenti e Decreti di Congregazione, 1540–1604'*, section relative to the *'Nota Decretorum Congregationis 1540–1604'*, references to 1571.

44 ASMP, *'Registro di Lettere Apostoliche ed Instromenti Diversi'*, c.73 dated 3 June 1539.

45 M. Tosi, *op. cit.*, pp.33–8.

46 D. Tamilia, *op. cit.*, pp.25 and 101; M. Tosi, *op. cit.*, p.34.

47 M. Tosi, *op. cit.*, p.35.

48 The half-yearly payment period is not based on explicit records but on the conclusions of M. Tosi, *op. cit.*, pp.33–6, and D. Tamilia, *op. cit.*, p.101. The payment amounts are my estimates based on the data in ASMP: *'Registro di Bolle, Brevi e Decreti di Congregazione'*, Tome I; *'Registri dei Decreti di Congregazione 1540–1566'*, Tome 39, part II; *'Registro di Lettere Apostoliche ed Instromenti Diversi'*. Up to 1541 the payment orders were

Notes to Chapter II

issued by the *provvisori* to the depositary (first Calciati, then Rucellai). Those for 1542 and 1543 were issued by the cashier, Angelo Antonio Tasca.

49 *Ibid.*, p.36. Tosi suggests that Crivelli raised the rent. This assumes the existence of a dual relationship between the Monte and the Crivellis, with the latter as both perpetual leaseholders (from the Ospedale dei Boemi) and lessors. Given the Monte's economic difficulties, this would not have been financially sustainable. In the absence of other data, I therefore assume that the Monte ceased paying rent for the building following the merger with the Ospedale dei Boemi in 1545.

50 M. Tosi, *op. cit.*, p.35.

51 ASMP, '*Registri dei Decreti di Congregazione, 1540–1566*', Tome 39, part II.

52 ASMP, '*Registri dei Decreti di Congregazione, 1566–1579*', Tome 40, entries dated 2 July 1567 and 10 June 1579. Tamilia identifies Piazza Catinara as the present-day Piazza Cairoli, which until the end of the nineteenth century was called Piazza di San Carlo ai Catinari. The move may well have reflected the Monte's fear that the dispute with the Boemi would force the Monte to give up the premises it leased. The end of the question, which marked the return of the Ospedale dei Boemi to full independence, was sanctioned by a brief issued by Pius V in 1572. D. Tamilia, *op. cit.*, p.102.

53 The congregation, chaired by the Cardinal-Protector Pietro Aldobrandini, approved buying the building on 21 October 1603. ASMP, Tome 13, '*Nota Decretorum Congregationis 1540–1604*', references to 1603.

54 ASMP, Tome 13, '*Nota Decretorum Congregationis 1540–1604*', references to 1558–80.

55 ASMP, Tome 13, '*Registri di Brevi, Instromenti e Decreti di Congregazione, 1540–1604*', section relative to the '*Nota Decretorum Congregationis 1540–1604*', references to 1562.

56 *Ibid.* This case was probably not without a cost to the Monte. The congregation's meeting of 2 April also approved requesting 2 *carlini* a year from all the members of the Company. This was the first subscription not limited to the delegates but extending to all the members of the Company.

57 See M. Tosi, *op. cit.*, pp.26–7. Also, ASMP, '*Inventario de libri e scritture del Sacro Monte di Pietà dal 1539 al 1634*', Tome 278, for references to the *Nota di libri e scritture che si trovano nell'archivio del Sacro Monte della Pietà, et appresso li officiali et ministri di detto Monte reviste et poste per ordine de' tempi dal Sig. Carlo Gabrielli, Deputato, come per decreto a dì 13 di Maggio 1603.* Gabrielli was able to consult the first book of loans and retrieved some information from it.

58 See D. Tamilia, *op. cit.*, p.74. The founding bull (ASMP, '*Registro di Lettere Apostoliche ed Instromenti Diversi*', p.148) notes that the Monte's capital consisted of a '*non parva*' sum of money.

59 ASMP, *Nota di libri e scritture…*, Tomo 258.

60 Tosi, who cites the limits on loan size, also raises the question of the doubtful dating of the text of the statutes preserved in Vatican Codex no. 6203, folio 150. Since the rules on loan limits probably only photographed the existing situation, it is entirely reasonable to assume that during the first period of operations (1539–65) the average size of loans was rather small (1–3 *scudi* was less than the monthly salary of an officer of the Monte). See Tosi, *op. cit.*, pp.51 and 81.

61 D. Tamilia, *op. cit.*, p.75, based on Gabrielli (ASMP, *Nota di libri e scritture…*, Tomo 258).

62 Bad debts not only exposed the Monte to the risk of capital loss when pledges were liquidated at auction but also strained its liquidity.

63 Gabrielli (ASMP, *Nota di libri e scritture…*, Tomo 258), D. Tamilia, *op. cit.*, pp.76–7, and M. Tosi, *op. cit.*, p.81.

64 The sources are notations in '*Registri dei Decreti di Congregazione 1540–1566*' (Tome 39) or '*Nota Decretorum Congregationis 1540–1604*'.

65 Average loan amounts are extrapolated from the figures found in '*Nota Decretorum Congregationis 1540–1604*', which are printed in bold. The hypothesised figures are in italics. According to Gabrielli, the Monte began lending on 28 April 1539.

66 Refers to the 32 years for which the number of transactions is known. If the 14 years for which the number is not known are included by assigning them an average of 3000 transactions per year, a figure of some 300,000 pledge loans is obtained for the Monte's first 45½ years of activity. Assuming an average of 2 *scudi* per loan, the total amount rises to the very substantial figure of 600,000 *scudi*.

67 Tosi, *op. cit.*, pp.41–2.

68 The congregation had actually begun to discuss charging 'just interest' as early as 18 May 1550, but it only reached a decision on 30 May 1552. ASMP, *'Registri dei Decreti di Congregazione 1540–1566'*, Tome 39, p.XV, c.29, and p.XXI, cc.41–2.

69 ASMP, *'Registri dei Decreti di Congregazione 1580–1593'*, Tome 41, 7 February 1584; see also D. Tamilia, *op. cit.*, p 75.

70 See M. Tosi, *op. cit.* pp.41–2.

71 The resolution was later confirmed. On 7 December 1575 the congregation ordered a new book of pledges to be prepared. The auction assistants were directed to keep a detailed record of the auction results, separately identifying those pledges that had not yet expired. They were to enter a summary description of each item, the price obtained and the earlier appraisal; these entries would then be checked against those of the cashier. The keeper of pledges was to be informed of the new procedure, in order to determine whether an annual audit should be performed. It was also decided that the Monte could cover the depository's shortfalls upon authorisation of the Monte's viscount-judge.

72 With a view to minimising the injury to borrowers in default, on 10 May 1540 the congregation laid down rules for the administration of pledges and auctions. Among other provisions, a period of 30 days was to pass before an item sold at auction could be delivered to the buyer, in order to facilitate late redemptions. However, the congregation abrogated this rule at its very next meeting on 11 July 1540. ASMP, *'Registri dei Decreti di Congregazione 1540–1566'*, Tome 39, p.III, c.5 and the first page of *'Registri di Brevi, Instromenti e Decreti di Congregazione, 1540–1604'*.

73 ASMP, Tome 13, *'Registri di Brevi, Instromenti e Decreti di Congregazione, 1540–1604'*, part relative to the *'Nota Decretorum Congregationis 1540–1604'*, references to 1569. Note that the cashier was not empowered to forgive any sum due from third parties without an explicit joint mandate of the two *provvisori* and was held personally responsible for any violation of this rule.

74 ASMP, Tome 13, *'Registri di Brevi, Instromenti e Decreti di Congregazione, 1540–1604'*, part relative to the *'Nota Decretorum Congregationis 1540–1604'*, references to 1570. Any down payment would be returned to the defaulting buyer. This rule, not particularly advantageous for the Monte, was apparently intended to make auctions more efficient.

75 ASMP, Tome 13, *'Registri di Brevi, Instromenti e Decreti di Congregazione, 1540–1604'*, part relative to the *'Nota Decretorum Congregationis 1540–1604'*, references to 1569.

76 See M. Tosi, *op. cit.*, p.41.

77 Lobbying efforts by the Monte were not confined to the official channel of the protector. The Company included many prominent members of the papal state's administration. One was the papal commissioner for the city of Rome, Antonio Lomellino, who served two terms as *provvisore* (1539–40 and 1552–4).

78 ASMP, Tome 13, *'Registri di Brevi, Instromenti e Decreti di Congregazione, 1540–1604'*, part relative to the *'Nota Decretorum Congregationis 1540–1604'*, references to 1568.

79 Running the depository must not have been easy. On 21 June 1575 we find the congregation discussing the 'damage and disorder due to the depository of pledges'. ASMP, Tome 13, *'Registri di Brevi, Instromenti e Decreti di Congregazione, 1540–1604'*, part relative to the *'Nota Decretorum Congregationis 1540–1604'*, references to 1575.

80 ASMP, *'Registri dei Decreti di Congregazione 1540–1566'*, Tome 39, p.II, c.3.

81 ASMP, *'Registri dei Decreti di Congregazione 1540–1566'*, Tome 39, p.II, cc.4–5.

82 ASMP, *'Registri dei Decreti di Congregazione 1540–1566'*, Tome 39, p.III, c.6.

83 ASMP, *'Registri dei Decreti di Congregazione 1540–1566'*, Tome 39, p.IV, c.7.

84 ASMP, *'Registri dei Decreti di Congregazione 1540–1566'*, Tome 39, p.IV, c.8.

85 ASMP, *'Registri dei Decreti di Congregazione 1540–1566'*, Tome 39, p.V, c.9. The two were Antonio Lomellino and Giovanni Arborino. Agostino Pessina was appointed keeper of the head office and depository (at the time located in the same building).

86 ASMP, *'Registri dei Decreti di Congregazione 1540–1566'*, Tome 39, c.11. Referring to the delegates, the source states *'videant computa D. Francesci de Galciati'*. See also ASMP, *'Registri dei Decreti di Congregazione 1540–1566'*, Tome 39, p.VII, c.13.

87 ASMP, *'Registri di Brevi, Instromenti e Decreti di Congregazione, 1540–1604'*, *'Nota Decretorum Congregationis 1540–1604'*, p.2. Referring to the new election, the text reads *'provisores ad menses sex'*.

88 ASMP, *'Registri dei Decreti di Congregazione 1540–1566'*, Tome 39, pp.VII–VIII, cc.14–15.

Notes to Chapter II

89   ASMP, '*Registri dei Decreti di Congregazione 1540–1566*', Tome 39, pp.IX, c.18, which states that the act was registered on Folio 276. The act was drawn up '*idibus martii 1546, 12°pp. N.S.*', or in the twelfth year of the reign of Pope Paul III.

90   Entries of the salary payments to the Monte's permanent officers ('salaried officials') show that from 1 July 1560 onwards the depositary handled such payments. The last entry for Algeziro dates from the beginning of May 1560.

91   ASMP, '*Registri dei Decreti di Congregazione 1540–1566*', Tome 39, p.X, c.20. '*Hora XX*' would correspond to the early afternoon.

92   ASMP, '*Registri dei Decreti di Congregazione 1540–1566*', Tome 39, p.XI, c.21.

93   The lack of references in this regard in the principal archival source (ASMP, '*Registri dei Decreti di Congregazione 1540–1566*', Tome 39, part II) is due to the occasional, discontinuous nature of the entries in the second part of the volume, which served mainly as memorandum items for resolutions of the congregation.

94   ASMP, '*Registri dei Decreti di Congregazione 1540–1566*', Tome 39, pp.XVII–XVIII, cc.34–5.

95   Source: ASMP, Tome 39, '*Registri dei Decreti di Congregazione 1540–1566*', and Tome 13, '*Registri di Brevi, Instromenti e Decreti di Congregazione, 1540–1604*', part relative to the '*Nota Decretorum Congregationis 1540–1604*', references to 1574.

96   An internal transfer bearing the same rate of interest as pledge loans, i.e. presumably 5 per cent.

97   ASMP, '*Registri dei Decreti di Congregazione 1540–1566*', Tome 39, pp.XVIII–XIXI, cc.36–7. The summary contained in the *decreti* for the meeting of 30 October represents a first concrete attempt to define structure and administrative rules of the Monte, superseding practices and rules largely dating back to period of the Monte's foundation.

98   They were Latino de Mantarco (Pigna district), Gabriele de'Vallati (Sant'Angelo), Giovanni Milesi (Parione), Vincenzo Margani (Campitelli), Marcello Maroncelli (Trastevere), Andrea Pelusi (Ponte), Bernardino da Pescia (also Ponte), Alessandro Bartoli (Regola), Gian Pietro Cardelli (Campo Marzio), Gian Maria de Tassi (Trevi), Paolo de Giunove (Colonna) and Gian Maria Franco (Sant'Eustachio).

99   Statutes of 1581, Chapters V, XIII and XXX.

100 ASMP, '*Registri dei Decreti di Congregazione 1540–1566*', Tome 39, pp.XXVIII, c.56. Earlier resolutions had not actually led to the production an official document. The Statutes laid down the following 16 fundamental rules:
- the new special committee meets fortnightly;
- a delegate must always be present at the time loans are disbursed and auctions held;
- the cashier must record the updated position of the treasury in a book each week;
- the cashier may disburse a loan only if at least one delegate is present;
- the assent of the accountant is necessary for a loan to be disbursed;
- the accountant must check the cashier's accounts each week;
- the custodian of pledges must report weekly to a delegate about the pledges sold and money collected;
- the custodian must sign a book of receipts at the completion of each loan;
- all *cedole* of deposits must bear the signature of the two *provvisori* and the accountant;
- the appraiser may not accept pledges except within the rules provided for in the papal bull founding the Monte;
- the appraiser may act only with the approval of the *provvisori* or, where appropriate, the congregation;
- officers of the Monte are prohibited from buying objects at the auction of expired pledges;
- an appraisal may not be amended without the explicit consent of the *provvisori*;
- all old pledges must be sold, and in the future no items will be kept for more than eight months;
- the custodian may receive a time commission on pledges realised, rounded to fifteen days or to the subsequent months (at least 20 days);
- the cashier may lend only with the approval of the congregation.

101 The source refers explicitly to specific cases reported in detail in folio 29 of the register of pledges (now lost). The rule in question was rigorously applied. On 20 July 1568 the congregation decreed that the cashier and custodian were obliged to indemnify the Monte for the losses of pledges for which they were to blame. On 1 March 1569 the custodian was ordered to pay the appraisal value of 16 items that had been lost. On 2

Banking and Charity in Sixteenth-Century Italy

April 1572 the congregation ordered payment to be made to the owner of an item that had been lost, without detriment to the Monte's position, and proposed taking action to ascertain the security of the depository and any responsibility on the part of officers of the Monte. ASMP, '*Registri di Brevi, Instromenti e Decreti di Congregazione, 1540–1604*', Tome 13, part relative to the '*Nota Decretorum Congregationis 1540–1604*', references to 1568, 1569 and 1572.

102   Some two decades later, on 14 February 1581, the congregation decided that the Monte would no longer agree to returning an item to an owner who had lost the receipt and could not supply proof of his right. Plainly, there had been cases of misrepresentation or fraud. In addition, the Monte's notary warned that an officer responsible for violating this rule would be held to refund the damage, plus expenses and interest. On 2 May 1581 the congregation laid down that only assets pledged to the Monte could be sold at its auctions, barring a waiver from the *provvisori*; in the event of such a waiver involving the sale of meat, any meat belonging to the Monte was to be auctioned first.

103   ASMP, '*Registri di Brevi, Instromenti e Decreti di Congregazione, 1540–1604*', Tome 13, part relative to the '*Nota Decretorum Congregationis 1540–1604*', references to 1571.

104   This was not the only decision of its kind. On 26 August 1575 the congregation deprived the *provvisori* and officers of the authority to return pledged assets to their owners without its approval and threatened to claim compensation for losses arising from infringement of the new rule; it advised selling the assets without delay in the event of default. On 15 November 1583 the congregation prohibited officers from pledging assets to the Monte; violators would be removed from office. That same day it made provision for further auditing, directing the cashier and the accountant to check each other's books. ASMP, '*Registri di Brevi, Instromenti e Decreti di Congregazione, 1540–1604*', Tome 13, part relative to the '*Nota Decretorum Congregationis 1540–1604*', references to 1575 and 1583.

105   ASMP, '*Registri di Brevi, Instromenti e Decreti di Congregazione, 1540–1604*', Tome 13, part relative to the '*Nota Decretorum Congregationis 1540–1604*', references to 1584.

106   See the text of the Statutes of 1581, preamble to the articles.

107   There is no record of early payments in the source, ASMP, '*Registri dei Decreti di Congregazione 1540–1566*', Tome 39, although this does not mean that none were made. For the period after June 1541 there is a detailed monthly record of payments (amount, number of employees, date, etc.). The names of the *provvisori* appear but rarely, usually only in the month coinciding with their taking office.

108   The cashier, Diego Algeziro, made the payments at the instructions of the *provvisori*. The payment orders were generally signed by the *provvisori*. Exceptions are those of 6 November 1551, 31 December 1551 and 4 March 1552, each of which was signed by two guardians.

109   ASMP, '*Registri di Brevi, Instromenti e Decreti di Congregazione, 1540–1604*', '*Nota Decretorum Congregationis 1540–1604*', references to 1565.

110   The permanent staff increased to four in January 1543 after a resolution of 10 January of that year instituted the position of accountant. From November the wife of the custodian, Agostino Pessina, was paid two *scudi* a month. Although her role was thus made official, she still was considered only the beneficiary of an extraordinary payment and not a permanent employee.

111   ASMP, '*Registri di Brevi, Instromenti e Decreti di Congregazione, 1540–1604*', '*Nota Decretorum Congregationis 1540–1604*', references to 1566. The same meeting also reinforced security, voting that there should be no more than two keys to the depository of pledged assets, one held by the custodian and the other by the depositary.

112   ASMP, '*Registri di Brevi, Instromenti e Decreti di Congregazione, 1540–1604*', '*Nota Decretorum Congregationis 1540–1604*', references to 1572.

113   ASMP, '*Registri di Brevi, Instromenti e Decreti di Congregazione, 1540–1604*', '*Nota Decretorum Congregationis 1540–1604*', references to 1572–8.

114   On European economic conditions in the period 1500–1700, see C.M. Cipolla, *Storia economica dell'Europa preindustriale*, Bologna, Il Mulino, 1974, pp.227–90; J.M. Kulischer, *Storia economica del Medio Evo e dell'Epoca Moderna*, Florence, Sansoni, 1964, Vol. II, pp.295–335; F. Braudel, *The Mediterranean and the Mediterranean World in the Age of Philip II*, New York, Harper & Row, 1972, second revised edition). The massive inflow of Spanish treasure initially spawned inflation while depressing investment, the latter notwithstanding the abundance of monetary capital and low interest rates. These

Notes to Chapter II

developments interacted with the intrinsic weaknesses of the system to produce a protracted recession and, in the long run, a fall in the level of prices and profits. Since precious metals were perceived as constituting 'wealth' and not a monetary instrument, the inflow from the colonies, theoretically making it possible to buy everything that one needed on the market, acted as a deterrent to productive activity. The consequent erosion of production led eventually to recession and to a flight of capital to 'hedge goods' such as land.

115 C. Manca, *L'economia mercantile marittima*, Padua, CEDAM, 1995. On the economic relations between credit, capital formation and development in rural economies, see O. Capitani, *Storia dell'Italia Medievale (410–1216)*, Bari, Laterza, 1986; M. Cattini, 'L'economia rurale in epoca preindustriale – proposta di un modello interpretativo', in *Dall'età preindustriale all'età del capitalismo*, Parma, Studi e ricerche dell'Università deglio Studi di Parma, 1977; idem, 'Problemi di liquidità e prestito ad interesse nelle campagne emiliane – Secoli XVI–XVII', *Studi Storici L. Simeoni*, XXXIII, 1983; G. Duby, *L'economia rurale nell'Europa Medievale*, Bari, Laterza, 1970; C. Klapish-Zuber and D. Herlihy, *Tuscans and Their Families: a Study of the Florentine Catasto of 1427*, Yale University Press, 1985 (Italian edition, 'I toscani e le loro famiglie. Uno studio sul catasto fiorentino del 1427', 1988); M.A. Romani, 'La carestia del 1590–93 nei ducati padani: crisis congiunturale e/o di struttura', in *Studi in onore di Gino Barbieri*, Salerno, IPEM, 1983.

116 On the situation in Rome, see A. Ait, 'Credito e iniziativa commerciale: aspetti dell'attività economica a Roma nella seconda metà del XV secolo', *op. cit.*; L. Palermo, 'Ricchezza privata e debito pubblico nello Stato della Chiesa durante il XVI secolo', *Studi Romani* vol. XXII, no. 3 (July–September 1974); A. Fanfani, '*Storia Economica*, pp.565–6. The number of loans granted by the Monte comes from ASMP, Tome 258, *Nota di libri e scritture che si trovano nell'archivio del Sacro Monte della Pietà, et appresso li officiali et ministri di detto Monte reviste et poste per ordine de' tempi dal Sig. Carlo Gabrielli, Deputato, come per decreto a dì 13 di Maggio 1603*, which states that 25,609 pledge loans were made in 1589, compared with 13,543 in 1584. Using the same source, Tosi reports that the number remained constant up to 1600. Tosi, *op. cit.*, p.87.

117 L. De Rosa, *op. cit.*, vol. I, p.18.

118 The case of the *monte* of Bologna has been studied in depth. See P. Antonello, *Dalla pietà al credito – Il Monte di Pietà di Bologna fra Otto e Novecento*, Bologna, Il Mulino, 1997, pp.23–86.

119 Although surviving source documents on that period tell us little about the size of transactions outside of pledge loans and some deposits, they do mention various types of financial transactions that were carried out, albeit occasionally, alongside core activity.

120 ASMP, '*Registri dei Decreti di Congregazione 1540–1566*', Tome 39, p.XI, c.21.

121 The privilege of 20 March 1548 applied to *monti* outside of Rome associated with the Company of the Monte, i.e. the body formed by those who had promoted the institution. The board was appointed by the Company and exercised all management and representative powers on its behalf.

122 This inaugurated retail commercial banking at the Rome Monte, which was actually among the last institutions of its kind to adopt the practice.

123 The formality justifying this process consisted in the fact that 'deposits' had taken the form of redeemable annuities. These had first been issued in connection with the promulgation of testamentary privileges. Whereas an effort had initially been made to encourage donations and bequests by threatening the nullity of wills that failed to provide for the Monte, over time it became standard practice to accept annuities made out to heirs as formal acts of the same value. The practice of paying interest soon spread to dowry deposits, surety deposits for litigation and finally ordinary deposits, which also took the form of annuities whose redeemability highlights their similarity to modern bank deposits.

124 As a rule, the allocation of resources raised was already determined when Rome public debt funds were set up; see F. Colzi, *op. cit.*, pp.2–64. It is worth recalling Marx's remarks in Vol. I of *Capital*: 'The public debt becomes one of the most powerful levers of primitive accumulation. As with the stroke of an enchanter's wand, it endows barren money with the power of breeding and thus turns it into capital, without the necessity of its exposing itself to the troubles and risks inseparable from its employment in industry or even in usury'. (*Capital*, vol. 1, Chicago, Charles H. Kerr, 1906, p.827.) The

debt of the Monte appears to have been sheltered from the 'troubles and risks' of industrial investment, and it was certainly protected from those of usury! However, the question remains whether it was actually transformed into productive capital.

125   See C.M. Travaglini, *op.cit.*, p.466; also ASMP, '*Registri dei Decreti di Congregazione (1633–1643)*', Tome 45, c.62, with reference to the board meeting of 11 March 1636. In reality, amounts of less than 30 *scudi* had been exempted from interest in 1615 and 1621 (see M. Tosi, *op.cit.*, p.87, referring to the 1617 version of the statutes published during the protectorate of Cardinal Pietro Aldobrandini). This may have reflected the change in economic conditions in Europe and possibly also renewed rigidity in the Church's position on the *monti* and usury.

126   The idea of interest as a 'value' of time preference was not clearly perceived in the economic interpretations underpinning the doctrine on usury. It was only remotely approached by the concept *lucrum cessans*, which in late Thomism was adduced as a cause of and possible justification for demanding a premium on the use of money. However, the idea of *lucrum* does not fit well with the modern concept of 'preference'. See among others M. Blaugh, *Storia e critica della dottrina economica*, Turin, Boringhieri, 1970, with an appendix by A. De Maddalena, who quotes Irving Fisher's 1907 definition of interest as an index of the community's preference for a dollar of present income over a dollar of future income (p.654). We should also note in passing that an institution designed to support essential consumption was useful to the papal government in order to curb popular discontent and lessen the risk of social revolt in an era of protracted recession.

127   Interesting reflections on this theme and on the social and economic implications of the application of religious rules to commercial activity are to be found in Weber's *Protestant Ethic and the Spirit of Capitalism*.

128   J.M. Keynes, *The General Theory of Employment, Interest and Money*, New York, St. Martin's Press, 1961, pp.351–2.

129   J.A. Schumpeter, *The Theory of Economic Development, op. cit.*, p.255 says: '...But no therapy can permanently obstruct the great economic and social process by which businesses, individual positions, forms of life, cultural values and ideas, sink in the social scale and finally disappear. In a society with private property and competition this process is the necessary complement of the continual emergence of new economic and social forms and of continually rising real incomes of all social strata. The process would be milder if there were no cyclical fluctuations, but it is not wholly due to the latter and it is completed independently of them. These changes are theoretically and practically, economically and culturally, much more important than the economic stability upon which all analytical attention has been concentrated for so long. And in their special way both the rise and the fall of families and firms are much more characteristic of the capitalist economic system, of its culture and its results, than any of the things that can be observed in a society which is stationary in the sense that its processes reproduce themselves at a constant rate'.

APPENDIX

Events and operations, 1539–84

The protectorate of Cardinal Francisco Quinones (1539–40): the founding of the Monte

The birth of the Sacro Monte di Pietà of Rome with the publication by Pope Paul III of the bull *Ad Sacram Beati Petri Sedem* on 9 September 1539[1] probably reflected Spain's diplomatic and political interest in the '*monte di pietà* model', but this is unproven conjecture. Less uncertain is the involvement of a group of prominent local and foreign merchants and aristocrats who as early as the first half of 1539, taking to heart the sermons of Fra Giovanni of Calvi, commissioner general of the Franciscans, had informally begun to conduct pledge-loan business in the spirit that would later distinguish the Monte.[2]

The chain of conjecture about Spain's political interest in the birth of the Monte is woven from the following:

- the Rome Monte was founded at almost the same time as its counterpart in Naples;[3]
- Cardinal Quinones, designated to be its protector, was without doubt the most influential Spanish prelate in Rome;[4] and
- the primacy of the Church's authority in matters of credit and business was being challenged everywhere by the Protestant Reformation, so that emphasis on the model of lending embodied by the *monti* may be viewed as a means of reasserting that primacy.

A further, perhaps politically less significant, element is that the *monti* arose as antagonists of local moneylenders, most of whom were Jewish, at a time when the Jews were being expelled from Spanish territory.

All this constitutes neither proof nor historical analysis, but the issues raised may help to frame and explain the events of 1539. The spirit of the endeavour was rooted in the Franciscans' fight against usury. And the Rome Monte does appear to have been the crowning achievement of a century-long effort. Its importance was underscored by the fact that the cardinal-protector of the Franciscans was also to be the protector of the Rome Monte. The latter duty thus fell to Cardinal Quinones, protector of the Franciscans and member of the titular clergy of the Basilica of Santa Croce in Gerusalemme in Rome (hence the appellation 'Cardinal Santa Croce'). Ultimately, the most plausible view is that the Rome Monte arose from the interplay between a spontaneous commitment on the part of a handful of Roman nobles to wage war on usury and a plan consciously pursued by the Church authorities, a reading that finds indirect support in the history of many similar institutions.

A recurring question is that of the real economic nature of the Monte in its early years of activity. Its transformation from a confraternity of charitable donors into a public entity fulfilling key functions in the field of credit was slow and gradual. In examining the Monte's early years we shall be retracing a process whereby a predominantly economic institution supplanted or was superimposed on a somewhat amorphous private association.

The first meeting of the delegates of the congregation of which we are certain took place on 11 April 1540 in the presence of Cardinal Quinones at the latter's palace in Rome. The meeting concerned organisational matters, above all the election of the Monte's administrative bodies.[5]

During the Monte's very first years it was customary to appoint the *provvisori* for three-month terms, but since the congregation met infrequently it was not uncommon for these officials to stay on after that term had expired. This is but one sign that the Monte was basically an informal institution whose workings were entrusted to the good will and sense of purpose of its promoters. Recognition of the criterion of administrative efficiency was only recognised, in theory, with the Statues of 1557.

The '*Registri dei Decreti di Congegazione*' mention two other meetings held during the protectorate of Quinones, one of which fell during the regency of Gaspare Contarini.[6] The role of Gian Giacomo Tassi, secretary of the Monte at its first meeting, deserves mention here. During his more than two decades in office Tassi drew up most of the summary records of meetings in his own hand, almost always in Latin.

The regency of Gaspare Contarini (July–November 1540)

The second meeting took place on 10 May 1540.[7] Its subject was a complex resolution on the administration of pledged assets and procedures for selling these in a way that would minimise the damage to defaulting borrowers.[8] Some of these decisions were amended at the next meeting. The session of 10 May was the first of many that would ponder how collateralised lending might be reconciled with charitable aims. It decided to introduce a grace period of thirty days for late redemption by the borrower before consigning assets to the buyer. This went together with a policy of remitting to the defaulting borrower any proceeds from the sale of his assets beyond what was needed to satisfy his debt, an approach adopted by virtually all *monti di pietà* and quite liberal by comparison with pawnbrokers' customary practice of keeping all of the proceeds from sales.

Cardinal Quinones fell ill at the beginning of the summer of 1540. The first page of the summaries of the congregation's resolutions, contained in the collection *'Registri di Brevi, Instrumenti e Decreti di Congregazione, 1540–1604'*,[9] tells us that the *provvisori* visited the cardinal-protector in July 1540 to report on the situation at the Monte. We can therefore surmise that Quinones continued to discharge his official duties until just before the third meeting of the congregation, which was chaired by Contarini. At that meeting, held on 11 July 1540, Giovanni Arborino and Corrado Grassi were appointed as *provvisori* and the discussion on the administration of pledged assets was taken up again. The congregation decided, *inter alia*, to abrogate the thirty-day grace period for the sale of goods.[10]

Cardinal Quinones died in November 1540, but not before placing the stamp of his stewardship on the institution. By contrast, Cardinal Contarini left no apparent trace on the Monte other than its association with his prestigious name.

The Monte during the protectorate of Rodolfo Pio di Carpi (1540–64): the transition from small charitable association to economic organisation

Cardinal Rodolfo Pio di Carpi was named protector of the Monte in late 1540, probably almost immediately after the death of Quinones in November. The importance of his two-fold role of protector of the Franciscans and head of the Monte almost certainly argued in favour of a short interregnum.[11]

Carpi's long tenure, spanning 24 years, saw the consolidation of the Monte and its slow transformation from an informal association of notables and clerics into a well-ordered institution governed by statutes and general rules of operation.[12] The period up to 1546, when the Ospedale di San Nicolò dei

Boemi was merged into the Monte, was one of gradual progress during which the cardinal sought to forge a stable, efficient organisation while fending off a host of economic difficulties.[13]

The new protector chaired the congregation for the first time on 13 January 1541.[14] At the beginning of his tenure the congregation met rather frequently. These gatherings took place at his palace in Campo Marzio and probably gave this group of wealthy merchants, aristocrats and high clerics an informal opportunity to discuss private business and the latest developments at the papal court as well as the Monte's affairs.

At the next meeting (on 29 March 1541) and the following ones the congregation began to trace out administrative and operational rules that ultimately would be incorporated into formal statutes.[15] The delegates directed the *provvisori* to name a deputy or substitute in the event of protracted absence, and appointed two delegates to verify consonance of operations with the spirit of the papal bull of 1539 and to report any breach.

The meeting of 2 May 1541 was the first one Fra Giovanni of Calvi attended and the occasion for his first official involvement in the Monte's administration.[16] Fra Giovanni must have been very welcome, for he brought with him a donation of 500 *scudi* from the King of Portugal and one of 100 from the Duke of Calabria, heir to the Portuguese throne.[17] These funds were transferred via a bill of exchange drawn on Rome.

The next gathering of the congregation, on 6 May 1541, centred on a substantial deposit of 500 *scudi* that was to be entrusted to the Monte and its new custodian, Agostino Pessina, at the explicit request of a deputy, Giovanni Nichelchim.[18] This was the first time the body took up a question relating to banking activity proper. The records do not indicate the terms of the transaction nor whether the deposit was to bear interest.

The congregation next met on 25 July 1541[19] and then on 18 April 1542 at the palace of Cardinal Pio di Carpi.[20] At the second meeting the delegates discussed the testamentary bequests of the 'rector of the Church of San Salvatore in Lauro', Antonio (de Ferrari), who before leaving on a pilgrimage to Santiago de Compostela had promised to leave a donation to the Monte in the event of his death and had named his brother, Cardinal Giovanni de Ferrari, executor. The cardinal, in his turn, had also undertaken to make a charitable donation. The delegates' concern in this matter centred on whether promises of future donations were acceptable. The same meeting also decided to have alms boxes for donations to the Monte placed in all the churches of Rome from 25 September.

The next meetings took place on 24 December 1542 and 10 January 1543.[21] At the late-December meeting, immediately adjourned to '*hora XX*' (around 3 p.m.) on some later date, it was announced that Gian Pietro Crivelli had decided to donate a house to the Monte. That building would be the Monte's headquarters at least until the merger with the Ospedale dei Boemi and perhaps beyond. It is not clear, however, whether the donation simply formalised an arrangement whereby the Monte already had use of a building near the Ospedale Boemo. The Monte's existing premises were situated 'in the place called the Chiavica opposite the Church of Santa Lucia'.[22] The latter can be identified as the Church of Santa Lucia del Gonfalone. (*Inter alia*, Crivelli is buried there.) The houses near the church were not far from the Monte's future headquarters at Palazzo Petrignani-Santacroce.

On 25 June 1543 the congregation discussed this very problem and appointed Angelo Massimo and Giacomo Crescenzi to find permanent offices for the Monte.[23] A month later, on 27 July, it elected Angelo Massimo and Giovanni Antonio Zoni as *provvisori* for a term of six months and voted to transfer the Monte's offices temporarily to the Monastery of Santa Maria del Campo, near the cardinal-protector's residence in Campo Marzio.[24] On 27 August there was further discussion of this move.[25] It seems the delegates hoped to delay it until obtaining formal assurances that the new premises would be available free of charge.

After a hiatus the congregation again met on 2 March 1544, with Fra Giovanni Calvi attending.[26] A short meeting was held on 25 February 1545 and the next one took place on 18 August 1545.[27] On the latter occasion the delegates voted to contribute loan capital, reflecting the emergence of operational difficulties and perhaps the weakening of the charitable zeal that had distinguished the institution's first years. The infrequency of meetings would bear out the latter hypothesis.

The merger of the Ospedale Boemo

On 6 December 1545 the congregation acceded to the Curia's proposal for the Ospedale di San Nicolò dei Boemi to be merged into the Monte pursuant to a papal decretal.[28] Bishop Boccaurato, the notary Francesco Baccodi and the two *provvisori*, Angelo Massimo and Giovanni Antonio Zoni, were appointed to negotiate the question with Cardinal Federico Cesi, protector of the Ospedale, and to offer him a pension of 200 gold *scudi* a year as compensation for the loss of his benefice.[29] This can be viewed as a direct intervention by the papal authorities to support the Monte at a time of difficulty. On 27 July 1546 the congregation formally ratified the union of the Monte with the Ospedale.[30] The contract was concluded on 15 March 1546 with an act drawn up by the notary Cinziolino de' Galosio and witnessed by Agostino Pessina and Antonio de' Galosio.[31]

This merger concluded the start-up period during which the Monte was basically a loose confraternity of patrons of charity. The question of its headquarters remained open, however, as did that of the need to consolidate its organisational structure by drawing up statutes. Decades were to pass before definitive progress was made in these directions.

An interesting aspect of this period of the Monte's life is the role of the most prominent members of the congregation, who were seriously committed to the institution's survival and backed their moral support with financial resources when the Monte's straitened circumstances so required. If it is realistic to think that idealism alone does not explain this, a plausible additional motive may have been linked to the quasi-banking activity in which the Monte engaged and its consequent far-flung network of relationships. For merchants and bankers such as Luigi Rucellai and Francesco Calciati, this must have been a strong incentive. The primacy of the Rome Monte made it a crossroads of relations that often led to important economic transactions. The years between 1546 and 1549 saw it gradually strengthen its position after turning the corner on the crisis of 1544–5.

Following the union with the Ospedale the cardinal-protector and the delegates bent their efforts to giving the Monte a stronger administrative foundation, a goal now within reach thanks to the marked improvement in the Monte's financial situation as a result of the real estate it had acquired. The first meeting of the congregation was held on 31 May 1547, nine months after ratification of the merger, and dealt primarily with administrative questions, including the appointment of a new cashier (Diego de Algeziro in place of Angelo Antonio Tasca) and a decision setting his monthly pay.[32] During this period organisational issues could finally take precedence over financial constraints, but the meetings of the congregation continued to be widely spaced. This may have been one reason why on 14 October 1547 the body decided that gatherings would take place at '*hora XX*' on the second

Tuesday of each month.[33] However, it is uncertain whether this rule referred to the full congregation in plenary meeting or whether the intent instead was to create a sort of executive board that would take care of business between general meetings. In the event, the congregation did not meet again until 20 March 1548, when it decided to apply to the pope for a general privilege: the financial situation had improved following the merger with the Ospedale, but the treasury was certainly not overflowing.[34]

The merger with the Company of San Bernardo

On the contrary, the period spanning the late 1540s and early 1550s saw further moves to raise funds from the congregation itself and finally the decision to merge the Company of San Bernardo into the Monte. The difficulties were due in no small measure to the persistence of the policy of interest-free lending, resulting in a permanent imbalance between income and outlays. Liquidity problems were frequent and extraordinary operations in respect of assets were necessary from time to time. The meeting of 20 March adopted several decisions concerning buildings owned by the Monte, principally with a view to improving property management and making assets more productive without diverting them from the charitable uses to which they had previously been assigned. These decisions mainly involved buildings that had come into the Monte's hands following the merger with the Ospedale dei Boemi.

On 10 July 1548 the congregation voted to petition the pope for a special loan from the Apostolic Chamber.[35] The impression is that the voluntary spirit continued to dominate day-to-day operations, despite the gradual progress towards forging a more clearly structured organisation. In the same meeting Giovanni Battista Tartaro was appointed *provvisore* and Giovanni Antonio Zoni was reappointed to the same office, Diego and Tranquilla Algeziro (husband and wife) were named cashiers and directed to make a surety deposit, and the procedure for keeping the accounts was specified, with the accounts to be entered in a book updated each month and available for inspection by the delegates.

In 1549 Carpi, about to leave Rome for the summer, proposed that the congregation designate Cardinal Santacroce 'regent' during his absence. The congregation did so on 26 May 1549, setting a precedent for subsequent regencies in the summer of 1551 and a period of several months in 1552.[36] Cardinal Santacroce chaired a meeting on 12 June 1549.[37] This was followed by another gathering at the Monastery of Santa Maria della Pace on 17 July.[38] Cardinal Santacroce's regency does not appear to have alleviated the Monte's financial difficulties, which were exacerbated by the policy of interest-free lending and the annual pension paid to Cosimo Ancaiano, and following Carpi's return the congregation began to review the question of loan interest.

The meeting of 18 May 1550 was the first of a series concerned mainly with the 'just interest rate' that the Lateran Council had confirmed was permissible in order to cover the expenses of lending[39]. The issue came up again on 6 June 1550 and 1 March 1551.[40] However, the time was not yet ripe, for the text of the summary of the meeting of 1 March explicitly states 'Nihil exigitur pro summa mutuata'.[41] In the end, the congregation would decide on 4 April 1552 that the hard-pressed institution, like many other *monti*, could not avoid charging 5 per cent interest in order to cover expenses.

The next meeting was held on 16 July 1551 under the chairmanship of the deputy protector, Cardinal Maffei, an important figure in the history of the Monte despite the brevity of his mandate (he only replaced Carpi for one summer).[42] The meeting was noteworthy for the decision to merger the Monte with the Company of San Bernardo, a richly endowed charitable institution that had had been founded by Francesco Foschi, a Roman aristocrat, as a kind of precursor of the Society of Saint Vincent de Paul. Its headquarters were in the Church of San Bernardo, which was demolished in the eighteenth century. (An altar dedicated to Saint Bernard in the Church of Santo Nome di Maria at the Forum of Trajan, built on the site, recalls the earlier church.) The Company was in the forefront in Rome in the fight against begging, granting board to the poor and indigent for at least two consecutive days.

On 13 August 1551 the representatives of the two institutions agreed to go ahead with the merger and to change the name of the Monte into the Monte di Pietà di San Bernardo.[43] Only a few months had passed, however, before the new name vanished and the old one reappeared in official documents. Tosi conjectures that a demerger took place after six months.[44] In the event, the merger had considerable impact on the Monte's activity, by injecting new assets and by extending its base of funding and support to the notables of the Company's congregation.[45] It is not clear whether the merger resulted from Cardinal Maffei's personal efforts or instead reflected more general concern in papal circles for the financial situation of the Monte. Like that with the Ospedale dei Boemi, the merger with the Company of San Bernardo came at a time of dire economic difficulty. Possibly, both mergers were attempts by the Curia to avoid allowing the Monte to lend at interest.

On the occasion of the merger with the Company the first statutes were promulgated, envisaging an organisational model apparently closely patterned on that of the Company: in place of the two *provvisori* the Monte was to have four 'guardian deputies', together with three delegates responsible for the accounts, a depositary general, a cashier and two permanent secretaries having the function of attorneys.

The Monte retained this structure until mid-1552, when it reverted to the traditional system of two *provvisori* assisted by the depositary, accountant and custodians. The appointments connected with the 'new course' were discussed on 30 October 1551 after Cardinal Pio di Carpi's return to active service.[46] In revamping the Monte's administrative structure, the congregation prepared operational rules that can be regarded as the first attempt to formalise the institution's arrangements in statutes.[47] The same meeting also appointed an assistant for the administration of pledged assets for each of the twelve districts of the historical centre of Rome.[48]

Considerable pains were taken to blend the two organisations, with appointments in the new Monte more or less equally divided between delegates of the Monte and members of the Company of San Bernardo. On 22 November 1551 a mass attended by all leaders of the Monte in the Church of San Bernardo further attested to the effort at union.[49]

There is little information on the period between late 1551 and early 1552, when the Monte was officially called the Monte di Pietà di San Bernardo. A meeting of the congregation on 14 February 1552, at the home of Cardinal Pio di Carpi, did not adopt any noteworthy decisions.[50]

Towards the first statutes

By contrast, the importance of the meeting of 4 April 1552 was underscored by the fact that it was chaired by Filippo Archinto, papal vicar for the city of Rome, and held at his palace.[51] The gathering initiated a complete overhaul of the Monte's administrative and operational structure and adopted decisions aimed at increasing the Monte's income from the buildings it owned, possibly with a view to a de facto divorce between the Monte and

Table XXI *Offerings personally presented on 3 May 1552 by officers of guilds in Rome*[52]

Donors	Amount (sc.)
Mercers	14.2.0
Stocking-makers	20.4.8
Carpenters	5.8.0
Barbers	4.4.3
Goldsmiths	10.0.0
Potters	8.7.0
Blacksmiths	8.0.0
Greengrocers	4.10.0
Saddlers	5.0.0
Company of Footmen of the Cardinal-Protector	6.6.0
Total	**87.5.11**

the Company of San Bernardo. Among its other decisions, the congregation approved a new policy of charging loan interest of 5 per cent for 'reimbursement of expenses', as allowed by the Lateran Council. Finally, it raised the question of new statutes, its interest no doubt having been catalysed by the short-lived reorganisation that had occurred during the merger. Five years would pass before a formal document was prepared; this delay indicates that the distinction between the Monte's twofold role of quasi-bank and charitable institution was still very blurred.

The years following 1552 were a period of great change, as the cardinal-protector and the governing body strove to improve the Monte's financial position and define stable organisational and administrative arrangements. Continual discussion of the institution's configuration and rules eventually led to the formal drafting of statutes in the meeting of 29 March 1557.

On 3 May 1552, in accordance with a decision adopted on 4 April, a procession was held at the Basilica di San Lorenzo in Damaso to collect funds for the Monte's activity. The guilds and companies that participated were primarily those of small craftsmen and tradesmen, suggesting that another goal of the initiative was to revitalise the Monte's 'popular' spirit. The results of the collection are shown in Table XXI.

If the appeal for funds was targeted at artisans and small tradesmen, this reflects the Monte's potential for providing support during hard times. Despite the stigma of insolvency that may have been attached to the small tradesman or craftsman who had to pawn goods at the Monte, the latter counted many 'working poor' among its borrowers. The decision to begin charging 'just' interest of 5 per cent was definitively ratified soon afterwards, on 30 May 1552.[53]

On the financial front, the chief initiative was a move to petition the pope and the apostolic administration to prohibit the Jews from holding auctions at the same time as the Monte. The problem of competing sales was constantly a matter of concern, mainly because the more liberal conditions that the Monte offered to defaulting borrowers made its sales less remunerative. The request for an 'exclusive right' to hold auctions on certain days may have been protectionist, but it was also very pragmatic and coincided with the papal administration's interest in safeguarding the prestige and operations of an institution of considerable economic importance for Rome. The Monte's officers and customers included high laity and clergy, and the constellation of interests revolving about it was expanding. A mixture of private institution and public entity, the Monte was becoming a crossroads of ever-closer ties between the Roman notables and the papal government, and often made loans to members of families well-represented in the Roman Curia. All of these factors, together with the Monte's social welfare role, motivated the call for a protected sphere. Nonetheless, the congregation's strenuous efforts still failed to square the accounts; fresh sources of funds had to be found.

On administrative matters, a plan was considered to set up a principal congregation to handle the affairs of the Monte and a committee for appointments. Ideas of this kind had been entertained in the past, but this time the intention was to enhance administrative efficiency by granting some operational power to the appointments committee and obviating the problem of protracted vacancies of office. However, the institution's ingrained inefficiency ensured that a structure resembling the 'executive committee' envisaged in 1552 was not created before 1557.

One year passed before the congregation next met, on 14 May 1553.[54] This gathering dealt mainly with administrative and organisational issues, a sign that the economic measures had not been ineffective and that the situation had grown less alarming. The congregation appointed a new depositary (Antonio de Maio), reappointed the two *provvisori* (Alessandro Bartolini and Antonio Lomellini), discussed the possible renovation of the

Monte's offices and examined questions concerning the assets and liabilities of the former Ospedale dei Boemi. The pledged assets in the Monte's possession were kept in several rooms in the main building of the Ospedale (which, it will be recalled, was situated next to the house where the Monte transacted business). These premises were wholly inadequate, and the congregation considered transferring the depository both for reasons of security and in order to avoid further expenses arising from the liens on that building.

The next meeting, held on 22 August 1553, was chiefly of an operational nature and discussed various deposits and other transactions.[55] In this regard, Tosi relates that deposits, including deposits of money, were formally accepted by the Monte, whose obligations were jointly and severally guaranteed by the members of the congregation.[56] Deposit-taking must have been more than a sideline or 'unofficial' business, for Tosi also reports that the Roman noblewoman Giulio Colonna was one of the very first depositors.

Acting on a proposal by the cardinal-protector, the meeting of 22 August appointed Alfonso Diaz to draft a brief memorandum on the indulgences and privileges established by the papal bulls regarding the Monte and, in particular, on the Rome Monte's relations with its counterpart in Bologna. Those privileges included the possibility for the Monte to place its collection boxes everywhere, not only in churches, and have them used without time limits, not only during mass. The memorandum also referred to the custom of not segregating testamentary bequests from the Monte's other assets. The impression is that of an attempt to resolve issues regarding the allocation of funds, possibly preparatory to codification of the Monte's administrative and management structure in statutes. With the steady development of the institution's activity, the redefining of operational and decision-making roles within its administration took on increasing urgency.

In the meantime, on 10 March 1555 the congregation elected new *provvisori*.[57] One was Gerolamo Guadagni, the other Donato Bonsignore, a merchant from Florence. In a letter, Bonsignore informed the congregation that existing commitments compelled him to decline the honour, whereupon the congregation replaced him with Alfonso Diaz.[58]

On 5 August 1556 the congregation, acting on a proposal by the cardinal-protector, finally established a sub-congregation with a formal mandate to assist the *provvisori* in ordinary administrative decisions.[59] The 'executive committee' that had been theorised over the years was born at long last. It was initially composed of four members of the congregation: Alessandro Bartoli, Gian Pietro Cardelli, Bernardino del Conte and Girolamo Guadagni. The delegation of powers appears to have been rather general, particularly as regards auctions and the administration of credit. There is little doubt that the cardinal-protector and the delegates intended the congregation to remain the Monte's supreme decision-making organ. Still, the four members of the committee were also instructed to prepare a first draft of official statutes to be submitted for discussion and approval to the 'general congregation', i.e. to an ordinary meeting of the delegates of the Company of the Monte. These statutes were the first official document defining the administrative and operating structure of the Monte; earlier resolutions of the kind had never led to the drafting of a set of such rules.

On Sunday, 16 August 1556, the new executive body held its first meeting at the cloister of San Girolamo alla Regola.[60] The discussion, which sheds light on the kind of tasks the four men had to perform, turned largely on the restructuring of the Monte's creditor positions, which must have included a large number of bad debts. The committee decided to renegotiate all non-performing loans except for the amount due from the custodian of pledges, Agostino Pessina. It also decided to estimate the hypothetical losses that would be incurred in the event that the pledged assets were sold at auction, i.e. to calculate the estimated realisable value of the collateral backing positions in default. After a lengthy debate on these issues, the body reviewed the first draft of the new statutes and decided to submit them to the next meeting of the congregation for definitive approval. However, that meeting did not take place until 29 March 1557.[61] A 16-point summary of the document is found in the *'Registri dei Decreti di Congregazione 1540–1556'*. On 3 April 1557 the first meeting of the new administrative committee, composed of four delegates and open to the *provvisori*, was held in the convent attached to the Church of San Salvatore in Lauro.

The final meetings of Pio di Carpi's protectorate

With the promulgation of the new statutes, the new executive committee took over many operating tasks and the meetings of the congregation grew less frequent. On 3 May 1557 it was decided to install a system of salaries set case by case and reflecting the actual workload, in place of the flat pay system in force up to then, which had aligned the Monte's salaries with those of similar positions at the papal court or Apostolic Chamber. In effect, in the late 1550s the payroll decreased substantially. The same session also discussed risk management measures and voted to hold the loan officer personally accountable if the value of pledged assets was insufficient to cover the loan they secured.[62] On 6 July 1552 the same subject came up again in relation to another group of assets that had to be put up for auction.[63]

The congregation's sessions, at least until the late 1550s and early 1560s, were increasingly devoted to administrative and management issues, at times limited to streamlining procedures and other minutiae. On 26 September, for example, it decided that a Pater Noster and an Ave Maria were to be said before every loan disbursement.[64] However, it occasionally addressed more substantive matters. On 27 January 1561 it decided to borrow 800 *scudi* at 8 per cent a year and on 4 October 1563 it discussed borrowing 900 *scudi*.[65]

Rodolfo Pio di Carpi died in 1564. During the last seven years of his life, coinciding with the period following promulgation of the new statutes, the cardinal-protector was far less active in the Monte's affairs than he had been in the early years of his protectorate. His successor was Cardinal Charles Borromeo, who already held a host of powerful offices, including that of Papal Secretary of State.

The protectorate of Charles Borromeo (1564–72)

The new protector's many duties prevented him from devoting himself exclusively or even primarily to the Monte. In the first meetings of the congregation after Borromeo took over, a major effort was made to put the administrative structure on a more efficient footing and rationalise the distributions of leadership and executive duties and responsibilities.

A start was made at overhauling the accounting structure and treasury audit procedures in the meeting of 14 August 1564.[66] On 27 June 1570 the accountant was ordered to prepare the annual accounts, 'to be discussed during the congregation', and on 5 September the cashier was ordered to report his balance at each meeting of the congregation. On 24 February 1571 instructions were given for an annual audit of pledged goods 'and of the Monte's money on their account' and for the preparation of annual accounts.[67]

Appointments of officers were regularly discussed by the congregation. For example, the appointment of Francesco Lavinio as custodian of the depository of pledged assets was decided on 23 January 1565. During the meeting of 5 February 1565 the new custodian made a surety deposit of 22 *scudi*. In the same meeting the new appraisers were designated.

On 25 March 1568 several new members of the Company were elected, including the Countess de' Carpi, a relative of the late protector, Atalante Celsi and Felice Tasca. On 7 September 1568 the security deposit for the cashier was set at 500 *scudi*. On 23 January 1571 Scipione Mancini was appointed custodian, with Carlo Niret and Ludovico Lante standing surety for him. On 21 February Alessandro Ciampoli was appointed accountant.[68]

The meeting of 3 September 1565 had capped the total credit exposure to any one individual at 3 *scudi*, probably more to avoid lending to persons not in need than for reasons of credit risk. On 17 September 1565 it was decided that the Monte's borrowings would bear interest of 6 per cent on principal of up to 500 *scudi*, 8 per cent on amounts between 500 and 1000 *scudi* and 9 per cent on amounts exceeding 1000 *scudi*, including legacies. These stringent limits were theoretical; in practice, the Monte often had to pay the going market rate for funds.[69] Limits on interest on the lending side were also set. On 23 September 1569 the ceiling of 5 per cent on pledge loans from the Monte was confirmed.[70]

The congregation also considered questions of administration and the distribution of tasks.[71] On 19 March 1565 two delegates were appointed to handle lending on Fridays, a practice that until then had been avoided. On 17 May 1565 the new *provvisori* were elected in the chapter hall of the Church of San Lorenzo in Damaso.

On 5 November it was decided that auctions should be held only on Wednesdays and Saturdays and never on holidays, and were to be attended by the custodians, the cashier and the accountant, with the obligation to book all the transactions. The congregation also ordered that this resolution be posted in Rome for the jubilee. On other occasions the congregation dealt with personnel administration. During Borromeo's protectorate, policy in this area was rather severe; on 13 August 1565 a ceiling of 2 *scudi* was set on the monthly salaries of the attorneys, cashier and custodian, well below the previous peaks of between 4 and 5 *scudi*.

A noteworthy decision was that adopted on 22 November 1569, when the congregation voted that goods bought at auction that were not paid for within fifteen days could be sold to others; any down payment by the first buyer would be lost. Although the cashier was not empowered to forgive any amount without the joint authorisation of the two *provvisori*, on 17 October 1570 the congregation instructed that if a buyer failed to come up with the money by the established day (and thus not necessarily within fifteen days of the auction), the owner of the goods could regain title by paying not the price agreed to by the buyer but that set by the appraiser. In this case any down payment by the buyer would be returned.[72]

Legal actions and disputes took up much of the congregation's time. For example, on 10 September 1566 nearly the entire meeting focused on a transaction in a dispute with Giovanni Strozzi. The session of 8 October 1566 was monopolised by the suit with Didaro Algeziro, the former cashier, and Brother Arcangelo Raymondi, a former *provveditore*. On 15 October 1566 the congregation gathered to discuss the 'suit for the Lante bequest in the hands of the Doria and Odescalchi'. The question appears to have been settled on 28 May 1567, although the record of the meeting of 6 June 1570 still mentions a 'settlement item with Lante'.[73]

The Monte's buildings were also frequently discussed. The session of 5 November 1566 examined a suit with Angelo Crivelli, son of Gian Pietro, one of the Monte's founders. On 27 October 1567 the dispute with Crivelli seems to have been settled. On 24 November authorisation was given for an action against Fulvio Theofilo, and on 22 December another transaction was approved, this time with Giacomo Gavilio, '*cum promessa de jure et de facto*'.[74]

The records sometimes reflect amusing incidents. On 22 September 1568 the delegate responsible for pledged assets was told not to accept foodstuffs, a stricture that was reiterated in January 1569. Two years earlier, on 15 October 1567, a legal dispute had been settled when an official swore that he had never received a quail as security for a loan.

Some of the formalities of religious observance were discussed in detail. On 17 September 1565 the congregation voted that the Company should meet at least once a year in the Church of the Santi Apostoli for a mass commemorating the deceased members of the confraternity. Similar entries are found on the occasion of the mass of 10 November 1567 and that of 4 November 1572. Other matters included the donation of candles to the pope and other authorities on special occasions. The session of

28 January 1568 voted to carry 'the candles to the pope' and, to mark the occasion, to allow sales but to forbid lending. On 19 December 1571 the congregation authorised spending up to 25 *scudi* for candles and other decorations to be given to 'the judge this Christmas'.[75]

The congregation often had to deal with relatively marginal questions concerning loan procedures or grants of authorisation to officers in matters of procedure and security. On 26 January 1568 it laid down that the proceeds from auctions should be kept 'in a separate place', that accounts should be reconciled on the same day and that the amount of any loan disbursed had to be booked and the depositary notified thereof.

On 3 February 1568 it stressed that the accountant and cashier always had to have access to the 'loan room'. On 29 December 1567 it ordered a general audit of the depository, and on 22 June 1568 it ordered that an inventory be taken of new pledged assets at least once a week and that the custodian receive 10 *carlini* each time for this work.

On 11 August 1568 three delegates were appointed – one each to supervise auctions, lending and collection.[76]

The new statutes for the birth of an efficient credit organisation

During Borromeo's protectorate a new and definitive text of the statutes was prepared. The issue was often discussed. A select meeting of 19 November 1565 decided to convene a session of the congregation to resolve on matters concerning the charter and statutes. On 20 May 1566 a meeting examined the bulls recently issued by Pius IV (probably the bull of 21 August 1560, published during the protectorate of Pio di Carpi).[77] On 7 March 1570 a first official version of the new statutes was laid before the congregation and it was decided to print a copy for the use of each officer.[78] The general congregation of 16 May 1572 approved the final version, including amendments regarding the administration of deposits and acceptance of guarantees and the chapters whose approval had remained pending.

On 17 August 1572 the congregation held its last session under the leadership of Borromeo at the cardinal-protector's residence. It was an occasion to draw a balance of a relatively brief period in which the Monte had made considerable progress. Borromeo was succeeded by Cardinal Giulio Feltre della Rovere, who took office in early 1573.

From 1572 until the conferral of the Deposit Bank in 1584

The protectorate of Cardinal Giulio Feltre della Rovere (1573–8)

During the interregnum following the end of Borromeo's mandate, administrative activity basically came to a halt. Until the end of 1572 the congregation met only once, on 23 December 1572.[79] Cardinal Giulio Feltre della Rovere, appointed protector in early 1573, served until 1578. The beginning of his term saw a new round of changes and adjustments to the Monte's ordinary administrative procedures. On 23 March 1574 it was decided that all the officers of the Monte could participate in its auctions and buy for own account in cash. However, goods bought by officers of the Monte had to be kept available for one month following the sale and in that space of time the original owner could redeem them by paying the same price that the officer had bid at auction.[80] Salaried employees were strictly forbidden to take part in the auctions.[81] Almost a decade later, on 15 November 1584, the congregation laid down that no officer could pledge any of the goods on deposit as security; violation was to be punishable by removal from office. The same day it ordered another audit of the loan and collection books, instructing the cashier and the accountant to check each other's books.

The congregation occasionally dealt with the settlement of legal questions and disputes regarding the Monte's operations. On 1 March 1573 it settled its differences with Lodovico Lante regarding the legacy of 1400 *scudi*. On 24 August 1579 it decided to seek a solution of the disputes regarding the deposit of goods subject to court-ordered seizure. These were delicate questions and had to be examined case by case. Accordingly, on 28 September 1579 it ordered a pledged asset to be returned, despite the seizure order, as the party that had sought the injunction approved.

Sessions often dealt with the handling of the accounts and administrative matters. On 16 June 1573 it was decided that the first meeting of every month would review the accounts of the cashier and hear a public report on all items from the accountant. Orders were also given to collate and summarise the plethora of items in the general accounting ledger into a new ledger and to prepare a summary balance sheet cleared of expired items.

On 26 October 1574 salaried staff were instructed not to accept orders not signed by at least one *provvisore*. On 10 May the congregation ordered that the amounts received in deposit were to be entered on a receipt at the time the deposit was made. In the

The protectorate of Cardinal Giulio Feltre della Rovere

absence of such a document, the cashier was not to accept deposits of any kind, although he could record multiple deposits on the same receipt provided the amounts were at least 10 *scudi*. This procedure was changed on 3 June 1578; thereafter each deposit was to correspond to a single document.

On 11 January 1575 Francesco Bonamici was appointed cashier. On 14 January 1575 the general congregation appointed three separate *provvisori* to the depository of pledged assets; the three were to be directly accountable to the general congregation. On 1 February 1575 Giacomo de Ricardi was elected cashier. On 17 February an order was given to pay the sums due to Alessandro Ciampoli. On 25 May Pope Gregory XIII created the depository of pledged assets and goods subjected to execution in judicial proceedings and entrusted it to the Monte di Pietà, a decision that turned the Monte into a quasi-governmental entity. The new duties must not have been easy, for on 21 June the congregation discussed 'damage and disorders' relating to the depository.[82]

On 26 August 1575 the *provvisori* and officers were stripped of the power to return pledged assets without the authorisation of the congregation. The prohibition followed a threat of a claim for indemnification for losses due to the conduct at variance with the new rule and with the guideline that collateral should be put up for auction upon default by the borrower. Rules were also established for the sale of jewels and diamonds: 'The custodian shall take them to the *provvisori*, and at least one of these and one of you delegates shall show them secretly to the appraisers, and one of these must attend the sale'.[83] From the tone of these instructions, one gathers that fraud had occurred. On 6 September 1575 note was made of a receipt granted to the custodian for a pledge he had consigned to the deputy protector. On 17 December the congregation ordered a new book of pledged assets to be prepared. The auction assistants were to record the results and mention any items that had not expired. Along with summary details of the items sold they were to record the price obtained and the earlier appraisal, thus making it possible to compare entries with those of the cashier. Finally, the custodian was to be notified of the new procedure, to assess whether it was appropriate to audit the holdings of collateral on deposit every year. On 19 August the limits on lending to individual customers was raised from 6 to 10 *scudi*; the rule against multiple pawning remained. On 31 January 1581 it was decided that the Monte could cover the financial needs of the depository upon authorisation of the viscount-judge (the officer of the Monte who judged cases to which it was a party). On 14 February 1581 the congregation laid down that goods would no longer be returned to borrowers without a receipt or other proof of entitlement; any officer violating this rule would have to make good the loss, plus expenses and interest. On 2 May 1581 it was decided that only collateral held by the Monte could be sold at its auctions unless a waiver was granted by the *provvisori*; if the third-party item was meat, it was to be sold after that of the Monte. The meeting of 5 December ordered an inventory of the depository to be taken and a book to be drawn up by 3 April 1582.

The protectorates of Cardinals Francesco Alciati (1579–80) and Filippo Guastavillani (1580–7)

On 19 August 1578 Cardinal Alberto Altieri was named 'prelate of the Monte'. He probably served unofficially as protector before that office was taken over briefly by Cardinal Francesco Alciati.[84] After Alciati's sudden death in 1580, the reins of the institution were taken by Cardinal Filippo Guastavillani, nephew of Pope Gregory XIII, who remained protector until 1587.[85]

The chief merit of the new protector was the publication of the new official statutes in 1581, but this does not mean that administrative matters received no attention. On 6 January 1582 the cashier was sacked, probably on suspicions of misappropriation of funds (the sources state that he 'has held in his hand more money than is usually held').[86] The cashier's designated successor, one Pietro de Fulviis, renounced the office but demanded compensation by the person chosen to take his place. Whether such compensation was actually awarded is not known. On 6 February 1582 the cashier's surety deposit was set at 2000 *scudi*.[87]

Financial questions were often on the agenda. On 6 March 1582 the Monte was asked by the papal administration to deposit with the papal depositary all the free funds kept at the Monte. This the Monte sought to avoid. The outcome of the case is not known. On 7 February 1584 the congregation voted to terminate the payment of interest on deposits. The rule may have been meant to apply only to future operations or it may have been retroactive and temporary, reflecting a temporary shortage of funds. Depositors claiming to receive interest payments due would be directed to appeal to the pope. However, on 10 April 1584 there was a discussion of accepting a legacy of 211 *scudi* made out to Maddalena, daughter of the late Vincenzo Anfossi, for her wedding day.[88]

As in the past, the congregation often discussed apparently formal or minor questions, such as the votive candles to be offered during Lent to the pope and a number of high prelates.[89] Matters relating to the buildings owned by the Monte and the problems arising after the return to the Company of the Boemi of the goods belonging to the Ospedale (1572) were frequently debated.

On 1 July 1578 the pope was asked to authorise the transfer of part of the Monte's activity to the Church of Sant'Agnese in Agone and that of Santa Brigida. On 17 February 1579 a transaction was proposed regarding some questions pending with the Boemi. On 10 June 1579 several members of the Company of the Monte were appointed to oversee the vacating of the old headquarters (probably the Orsini Palace in Piazza Catinara) and assist the removal to the new headquarters, in the street 'called Campidoglio della Compagnia del Gesù'.[90]

On 7 July 1579 authorisation was given for the keys of the old headquarters to be returned to Orsini's agents. On 20 December a meeting took up a number of administrative questions and resolved to petition the pope concerning developments with regard to the headquarters and to the settlement with the Boemi.

The protectorate of Guastavillani saw the long and intricate question of the statutes draw to a conclusion with publication of the document in 1581.[91] With the final enactment of the statutes, the Monte completed its transition. Its new status was consecrated on 1 October 1584 with the papal brief *'inter multiplices'* entrusting the Monte with the Bank of Deposits and transforming it into a state bank.

Notes

1 ASMP, *'Registro di Bolle, Brevi e Decreti di Congregazione'*, Tome I, c.33, the bull *Ad Sacram Beati Petri Sedem*.

2 According to Tosi, *op. cit.*, pp.26-7, operations commenced on 2 April 1539 in a shop made available by the Milanese merchant Giovanni Pietro Crivelli. See also ASMP, *Nota di libri e scritture...*, the note concerning the Monte's archive drafted on 13 May 1603 by Carlo Gabrielli, who had been able to consult the Monte's now-lost first loan book. D. Tamilia, *op. cit.*, reports that Giovanni of Calvi (or Calvo), born Giovanni Maltei, a native of Corsica, was a major figure in promoting the Rome Monte. According to Tamilia, Fra Giovanni was appointed 'definitor general' in the Nice chapter of the Franciscan order in 1535, commissioner general at the Roman Curia in 1538, and superior general in the order's Mantua chapter in 1541. Citing Wadding's *Annales Minorum* (Tome XVIII), he relates that Fra Giovanni died in 1547, possibly after a journey to Portugal. According to Tosi, *op. cit.*, p.31, Fra Giovanni died of plague in early 1547 during the proceedings of the Council of Trent.

3 The Kingdom of Naples belonged to Charles V but it was also a traditional vassal state of the papacy. This relationship was acknowledged every year with payment to the papacy of the symbolic tribute of one horse.

4   Francisco Quinones, former superior general of the Franciscans, was made a cardinal by Pope Clement VII after acting as the pope's ambassador in peace negotiations with Charles V following the sack of Rome in 1527. (Quinones would later be Charles's confessor.) Until 1531 he was protector of the emperor's interests at the Holy See. Subsequently, until his death, Quinones was a member of the Company of San Gerolamo della Carità, protector of the Order of Franciscans and an authoritative representative of the Spanish clergy before the pope. In 1535 Quinones drew up the important new Roman Breviary.

5   ASMP, '*Registri dei Decreti di Congregazione 1540–1566*', Tome 39, p.II, c.3, begins: '*Congregati in sala Rev. D.F. della S.ta Cruce, S.R.E. pretis cardinalis et infraquibus deputati et officiales Sacri Monti Pietatis de Urbe*'. The names of the participants follow: Pietro Vorsio, bishop of Aquino, Giovanni Arborino, apostolic gonfalonier, Antonio Lomellino, apostolic protonotary, Tomaso de Taini, hearer of cases at the Holy Palaces, Luigi de' Torres, apostolic scriptor, Corrado Grassi, Giovanni Marsia, Giovanni Antonio Zoni, Giovan Pietro Crivelli of Milan, the Florentine merchant Luigi de Rucellai, the Roman noblemen Angelo de Massimo and Giacomo de Crescenzi, the Milanese merchant Francesco de' Galciati, and the notaries Francesco Baccodi and Giovanni Triolati. Massimo, Rucellai and Calciati were appointed to keep the accounts, Calciati was entrusted with the treasury until the end of 1540 and Lomellino and Crescenzi were appointed *provveditori* for three months. Gian Giacomo Tassi, appointed secretary of the Monte, was entrusted with drawing up the minutes (including those of the meeting of 11 April 1540).

6   Contarini (1483–1542), born in Venice, had spent his youth studying in Padua. In 1516 he wrote *De Officiis Episcopi*, a handbook for bishops. In 1535 Contarini was made a cardinal even though he had not yet been ordained a priest, and in 1536 he was assigned the bishopric of Belluno. In 1537 he was part of a committee of cardinals appointed to present Paul III a document on the reform of the Church, *Consilium de emendanda Ecclesia*. Very active in seeking reconciliation with the Protestants, in 1540 Contarini took part in the colloquies at Speyer and Worms preparatory to the Diet of Regensburg. Soon afterwards he was asked to stand in for the ailing Quinones at the Rome Monte.

7   ASMP, '*Registri dei Decreti di Congregazione 1540–1566*', Tome 39, p.II, c.4. The meeting was chaired by Quinones. Participating were Giovanni Arborino, *provvisore*, Giacomo de' Crescenzi, Corrado Grassi, Rocco de' Cenci, Giovanni Antonio Zoni, Luigi Rucellai, Giovanni Marsia, Francesco Galciati and Francesco Baccodi. The meeting also appointed Crescenzi to supervise the appraisal of pledged assets and conferred more detailed operational duties on the *provvisori*. (These steps, tentative and not reflecting part of a clear organisational plan, would be followed by unending adjustments.) The notary Francesco Baccodi notified the other participants of the content of a papal bull on the ideals and principles underpinning the functioning of the Monte. Also, it was decided to appoint a permanent custodian of the Monte's depository and headquarters.

8   The organisation of lending remained basically unchanged until 1552, when the Lateran Council's line concerning interest on loans was finally adopted. Until that time the Monte even refrained from charging interest disguised as 'reimbursement of expenses'. Goods to be pledged were appraised and loans disbursed every Monday and Friday and always in the presence of at least two delegates. Borrowers could redeem pledges within six months, after which their goods were included in the list of items to be sold at the next auction. If the proceeds from the sale exceeded the amount of the loan, the difference, following the extinguishing of every obligation, was handed over to the borrower.

9   ASMP. This contains summaries of salient aspects of the Monte's administration and a detailed list of the resolutions adopted by each meeting of the congregation during the period in question. It is valuable for cross-checking against the '*Registri dei Decreti di Congregazione*' (Tomes 39–41), which contain the minutes giving a fuller description of the resolutions.

10 ASMP, '*Registri dei Decreti di Congregazione 1540–1566*', Tome 39, p.III, c.5. Participating were Cardinal Contarini, Pietro Vorsio, Tomaso Taini, auditor of the rota, Giovanni Arborino, Giovanni Marsia, Giovanni Antonio Zoni, Francesco Baccodi, Giacomo Crescenzi, Gian Pietro Troylati, Gian Pietro Crivelli, Angelo Massimo, Francesco Galciati, Luigi de Torres, Corrado Grassi, Francesco Vannutio and

Notes to Appendix

Bernardo Santacroce. The last-mentioned does not appear to have been related to Quinones, but was instead a member of the Roman family whose palace has served as the Monte's headquarters since the late 1500s. Revocation of the earlier decision is confirmed by the first page of '*Registri di Brevi, Instromenti e Decreti di Congregazione, 1540–1604*'. Most probably, the grace period had proved too short to be of any real help to indigent borrowers but long enough to be an impediment to the ready liquidation of the goods held by the Monte, discouraging buyers, tending to depress prices and putting the Monte at a disadvantage in its rivalry with the Jewish moneylenders, whose auctions did not place such limitations on the rights of buyers.

11   In ASMP, '*Registri dei Decreti di Congregazione 1540–1566*', Tome 39, he is habitually referred to simply as 'Rodolfo Cardinal Carpi'. D. Tamilia, *op. cit.*, never identifies him as a member of the well-known Pio family. Tosi, *op. cit.*, pp.42–3, marshals convincing evidence identifying the new protector as Rodolfo Pio di Carpi, cardinal of the titular clergy of Santa Prisca. Carpi was a major figure of his day. Upon Carpi's death in 1564, Pope Pius V had the epigraph 'Defender of the rights of the Church, born for charity' inscribed on his funeral stone in the Church of Trinità dei Monti. Carpi served in the dual role of protector from 1540 until 1564. He lived for many years in Rome, where he had a villa on the Quirinal known for its gardens (the 'Orti Carpensi') and a palace in Campo Marzio. After 1564 the palace was temporarily the residence of the new Roman Seminary, which Carpi himself had founded. Like Quinones before him, Carpi served for a time as protector of Emperor Charles V's affairs at the Holy See, lending further weight to the hypothesis of a Spanish imperial interest in the Rome Monte or even in the *monti di pietà* in general.

12   ASMP, '*Registro di Lettere Apostoliche ed Instromenti Diversi*', p.148, evidences that the Company of the Monte had 941 members in 1542. By the end of the century its members numbered some 2000 (M. Tosi, *op, cit.*, ch.IV).

13   Cardinal Pio di Carpi no doubt was comforted by the aid of Fra Giovanni of Calvi, who attended two meetings of the congregation in 1541 and one in 1544. These were the only occasions on which Fra Giovanni was officially involved in the Monte's administration. The records refer to him as, alternatively, '*Ordo S.ti Francisci generalis*', '*Rev. padre generale*' and '*Commissario Generale dell'ordine*'. ASMP, '*Registri dei Decreti di Congregazione 1540–1566*', Tome 39.

14   ASMP, '*Registri dei Decreti di Congregazione 1540–1566*', Tome 39, p.III, c.6. Participating were Cardinal Pio di Carpi, Antonio Lomellino, apostolic protonotary, Giovanni Arborino, Luigi de Torres, apostolic secretary, Corrado Grassi, Francesco Vannutio, Bishop Gerolamo Boccaurato ('episcopus Arionensis'), Giovanni Antonio Zoni, Tomaso Guerri, Gian Pietro Crivelli, Giacomo Crescenzi, Angelo Massimo, Francesco Calciati, Luigi Rucellai, Francesco Baccodi and Gian Pietro Troylati. Apart from the cardinal's pledge to donate 3 *scudi* a month to the Monte, the meeting dealt with administrative affairs: Francesco Vannuzio and Giovanni Antonio Zoni were appointed *provvisori* for a term of three months, Francesco Calciati was appointed depositary; Gerolamo Boccaurato and Luigi Rucellai were named 'auditors of the accounts'; and Rucellai received solemn confirmation that the Monte would repay a sum of money that he had advanced on its behalf.

15   ASMP, '*Registri dei Decreti di Congregazione 1540–1566*', Tome 39, p.IV, c.8. Participating were Cardinal Pio di Carpi, Antonio Lomellino, Giovanni Zoni, Giovanni Arborino, Luigi de Torres, Corrado Grassi, Tomaso Taini, Gerolamo Boccaurato, Gian Pietro Crivelli, Giacomo Crescenzi, Francesco Calciati, Francesco Baccodi, Gian Pietro Troylati and Desiderio de' Auditorio.

16   ASMP, '*Registri dei Decreti di Congregazione 1540–1566*', Tome 39, p.IV, c.8. Participating were the Cardinal Carpi, Fra Giovanni, Ludovico de Torres, Giovanni Arborino, Antonio Lomellino, Corrado Grassi, Giovanni Antonio Zoni, Francesco Vannutio, Gerolamo Boccaurato, Tomaso Guerri, Gian Pietro Crivelli, Luigi Rucellai, Giacomo Crescenzi, Francesco Calciati, Desiderio de' Auditorio, Antonio Milesi and Rocco de' Cenci. The congregation renewed the mandates of the two delegates who had been designated in January for another three months, awarded the appraiser of pledged assets a yearly salary of 25 *scudi* payable in monthly instalments, and set the pay of the custodians of pledged assets at 40 *scudi* a year.

17   ASMP, '*Registri di Brevi, Instromenti e Decreti di Congregazione, 1540–1604*', '*Nota Decretorum Congregationis 1540–1604*', p.2, states '*a rege Portugalli*', whereas the text in '*Registri*

dei Decreti di Congregazione 1540–1566', Tome 39, p.V, c.9, speaks only of the 'Serenessimo Rege' without identifying him.

18 ASMP, 'Registri dei Decreti di Congregazione 1540–1566', Tome 39, p.V, c.9. Participating were Antonio Lomellino, Tomaso Taini, Giovanni Antonio Zoni and Agostino Pessina. Antonio Lomellino and Giovanni Arborino were elected appraisers, while Pessina was appointed custodian of the head office and depository of pledges (then located in the same building). The deposit, probably a surety deposit for the appraisers, is referred to in ASMP, 'Registri di Brevi, Instromenti e Decreti di Congregazione, 1540–1604', 'Nota Decretorum Congregationis 1540–1604', p.2.

19 ASMP, 'Registri dei Decreti di Congregazione 1540–1566', Tome 39, p.V, c.9. Participants: Cardinal Carpi, Fra Giovanni of Calvi, Luigi de' Torres, Giovanni Arborino, Antonio Lombellino, Gherardo Grassi, Giovanni Antonio Zoni, Francesco Vannutio, Tomaso Guerri and Luigi Pomarario, Luigi Rucellai, Angelo Massimo, Giacomo Crescenzi and Francesco Calciati. The meeting elected Massimo and Rucellai *provvisori*, approved the statement of account drawn up by the depositary Francesco Calciati and named Rucellai to replace Calciati as delegate responsible for keeping the accounts.

20 ASMP, 'Registri dei Decreti di Congregazione 1540–1566', Tome 39, p.V, c.10, contains the note for the meeting bearing the signature of Gian Giacomo Tassi.

21 ASMP, 'Registri dei Decreti di Congregazione 1540–1566', Tome 39, p.V, c.10 for the former. Participants: Cardinal Pio di Carpi, Luigi de Torres, Giovanni Antonio Zoni, Francesco Vannutio, Gerolamo Boccaurato, Lorenzo de Castello, Luigi Rucellai and Gian Piero Troylati. ASMP, 'Registri dei Decreti di Congregazione 1540–1566', Tome 39, p.V, c.11 for the latter. Participants: Cardinal Carpi, Fra Girario, former procurator general of the Franciscans, Luigi de' Torres, Giovanni Arborino, Antonio Lomellino, Giovanni Antonio Zoni, Gerolamo Boccaurato, Lorenzo de Castello, Gian Piero Crivelli, Luigi Rucellai, Angelo Massimo, Giacomo Crescenzi, Francesco Baccodi, Gian Pietro Troylati and Desiderio de Auditorio. The meeting elected Castello and Boccaurato *provvisori*, named Rucellai depositary and set the annual salary (30 *scudi*) and tasks of the accountant ('*computista*').

22 ASMP, 'Registro di Lettere Apostoliche ed Instromenti Diversi', c.73, instrument dated 3 June 1539.

23 ASMP, 'Registri dei Decreti di Congregazione 1540–1566', Tome 39, p.VI, c.12. Participants: Cardinal Carpi, Antonio Lomellino, Giovanni Antonio Zoni, Tommaso Taini, Lorenzo de Castello, Gian Piero Crivelli, Luigi Rucellai, Angelo Massimo, Giacomo Crescenzi, Gian Pietro Troylati, Desiderio de Auditorio and Rocco de' Cenci. The meeting also discussed the donations collected in the alms boxes placed in churches throughout the city.

24 ASMP, 'Registri dei Decreti di Congregazione 1540–1566', Tome 39, p.VII, c.13. Participants: Cardinal Carpi, Giovanni Arborino, Antonio Lomellino, Giovanni Antonio Zoni, Francesco Vannutio, Tomaso Guerri, Lorenzo de Castello, Luigi Rucellai, Angelo Massimo, Giacomo Crescenzi, Gian Pietro Troylati and Desiderio de Auditorio. Evidence of the six-month term is found in 'Registri di Brevi, Instromenti e Decreti di Congregazione, 1540–1604', 'Nota Decretorum Congregationis 1540–1604', p.2.

25 ASMP, 'Registri dei Decreti di Congregazione 1540–1566', Tome 39, p.VII, c.14. Participants: Cardinal Carpi, Giovanni Arborino, Antonio Lomellino, Tomaso Taini, Giovanni Antonio Zoni, Francesco Vannutio, Angelo Massimo, Giacomo Crescenzi, Francesco Baccodi and Desiderio de Auditorio. In contrast with the above source, the evidence in 'Registri di Brevi, Instromenti e Decreti di Congregazione, 1540–1604', 'Nota Decretorum Congregationis 1540–1604', p. 2, notes the congregation's desire to have the new headquarters free of charge.

26 ASMP, 'Registri dei Decreti di Congregazione 1540–1566', Tome 39, pp.VII–VII, cc.14–15. Participants: Cardinal Carpi, Fra Giovanni, Giovanni Arborino, Antonio Lomellino, Giovanni Antonio Zoni, Francesco Vannutio, Gerolamo Boccaurato, Tomaso Guerri, Lorenzo de Castello, Luigi Rucellai, Angelo Massimo, Francesco Baccodi and Desiderio de' Auditorio.

27 ASMP, 'Registri dei Decreti di Congregazione 1540–1566', Tome 39, p.VIII, c.15, does not list the names of the participants but mentions that the cardinal-protector was present and notes that the meeting was aborted almost at once. The participants in the meeting of 18 August are listed in ASMP, 'Registri dei Decreti di Congregazione 1540–1566', Tome 39, p.VIII, c.16, as Cardinal Carpi, Luigi de' Torres, Antonio Lomellino, Giovanni

Notes to Appendix

Antonio Zoni, Tomaso Taini, Gerolamo Boccaurato, Lorenzo de Castello, Gian Piero Crivelli, Luigi Rucellai and Angelo Massimo.

28 ASMP, '*Registri dei Decreti di Congregazione 1540–1566*', Tome 39, p.IX, c.17. Participants: Cardinal Carpi, Antonio Lomellino, apostolic protonotary, Gerolamo Boccaurato, bishop, Francesco Vannuzio, canon of Saint Peter's, Giovanni Arborino, canon of Saint Peter's, Pietro Vorsio, bishop of Aquino, Luigi de' Torres, apostolic secretary, Desiderio de' Auditorio, Angelo Massimo, Giovanni Antonio Zoni, Francesco Baccodi, Gian Piero Crivelli, and Gian Giacomo Tassi, who signed the minutes. M. Tosi, *op. cit.*, asserts that the name of the hospital was San Ladislao or San Venceslao, but the name San Nicolò clearly appears in the '*Registri dei Decreti di Congregazione*', p.IX, c.18).

29 ASMP, '*Registri di Brevi, Instromenti e Decreti di Congregazione, 1540–1604*', '*Nota Decretorum Congregationis 1540–1604*', p. 2. Perhaps because his title to the benefice was purely formal, Cardinal Cesi was expected to remit the pension to the rector of the Ospedale, Cosimo Ancaiano (or Ancaini), and the latter's assistant, Martino Poloni.

30 ASMP, '*Registri dei Decreti di Congregazione 1540–1566*', Tome 39, p.IX, c.18. Participants: Cardinal Carpi, Antonio Lomellino, apostolic protonotary, Gerolamo Boccaurato, bishop, Francesco Vannuzio, canon of Saint Peter's, Luigi de' Torres, apostolic secretary, Angelo Massimo, Giovanni Antonio Zoni, Francesco Baccodi, Gian Piero Crivelli and Gian Giacomo Tassi, who signed the minutes.

31 ASMP, '*Registri dei Decreti di Congregazione 1540–1566*', Tome 39, p.IX, c.18. The act was registered on Folio 276 and dated '*idibus martii 1546, 12°pp.N.S.*', i.e. the twelfth year of the reign of Pope Paul III. The contract provided for the Monte to pay a life pension of 200 gold *scudi* a year to the rector of the Ospedale, Cosimo Ancaiano. This pension became a heavy burden on the Monte's treasury and the Monte endeavoured repeatedly to extinguish the obligation. The merger nonetheless brought the Monte immediate financial relief and a very substantial portfolio of real estate. It also spawned a running dispute between the priests attached to the Ospedale (Ancaiano and Martino Poloni) and the officials of the Monte. In 1572 Pius V decided to undo the merger, restoring the Ospedale's independence (see M. Tosi, *op. cit.*, pp.37–8).

32 ASMP, '*Registri dei Decreti di Congregazione 1540–1566*', Tome 39, p.X, c.19. Participants: Cardinal Carpi, Luigi de' Torres, Antonio Lomellino, Giovanni Antonio Zoni, Francesco Vannunzio, Gian Pietro Crivelli, Angelo Massimo, Francesco Baccodi, Gian Giacomo Tassi, Andrea Pelusi, Andrea Carillo and Didaro (or Diego) Algeziro. The latter's given name generally appears as 'Diego' where the text is in Italian or a hybrid of Italian and Latin and as 'Didaro' where it is in proper Latin.

33 ASMP, '*Registri dei Decreti di Congregazione 1540–1566*', Tome 39, p.X, c.20. Participants: Cardinal Carpi, Luigi de' Torres, Giovanni Antonio Zoni, Gian Pietro Crivelli, Angelo Massimo, Francesco Baccodi and Agostino Pessina. Cf. ASMP, '*Registri di Brevi, Instromenti e Decreti di Congregazione, 1540–1604*', '*Nota Decretorum Congregationis 1540–1604*', p.3, where the decision is motivated by the need to attend to the Ospedale's assets and properties. The same meeting also discussed the annual pension of 200 *scudi* payable to the former rector of the Ospedale, Cosimo Ancaiano. A series of steps were planned to raise the required funds. If these failed, Cardinal Farnese was to be asked to intercede with the pope on the Monte's behalf.

34 ASMP, '*Registri dei Decreti di Congregazione 1540–1566*', Tome 39, p.XI, c.21. Participants: the cardinal-protector, Luigi de' Torres, Giovanni Antonio Zoni, Francesco Vannunzio, Msgr Vicenzo Scifola, bishop of Mirandola and Gerapoli, Gian Giacomo Tassi, Angelo Massimo, Francesco Baccodi, Andrea Carillo, Gian Mario de' Tassi and Andrea Pelusi. General privileges were common among *monti di pietà* in Italy. They were normally promulgated by the local ecclesiastical authorities and accompanied indulgences and other measures of support. The relatively late date at which this step was taken may have been due to the fact that the application was addressed to the Roman Curia and thus required scrupulous preparation. An awareness of the wider implications of any measure involving the Rome Monte may also have been a factor. But it is also quite possible that the delay was due simply to the informal and precarious nature of the Monte's early organisation. Arguably, the institution's financial difficulties should have spurred the papal authorities to do whatever could be done (at the lowest possible cost) to assist the Monte without deflecting it from its original social and charitable aims.

35   ASMP, '*Registri dei Decreti di Congregazione 1540–1566*', Tome 39, p.XI, c.22. Participants: the cardinal-protector, Luigi de' Torres, Antonio Lomellino, Giovanni Antonio Zoni, Francesco Vannunzio, Lorenzo de' Castello, Lorenzo Virilio, Gian Pietro Crivelli, Giovanni Battista Tartaro, Francesco Baccodi, Gian Mario de' Tassi, Andrea Carillo and Giovanni Guadagni.

36   ASMP, '*Registri dei Decreti di Congregazione 1540–1566*', Tome 39, p.XIII, c.25. Participants: Cardinal Pio di Carpi, Giovanni Arborino, Giovanni Antonio Zoni, Francesco Vannunzio, Bishop Scifola, Gian Pietro Crivelli, Francesco Baccodi, Andrea Carillo, Giovanni Battista Tartaro and Giovanni Guadagni.

37   ASMP, '*Registri dei Decreti di Congregazione 1540–1566*', Tome 39, p.XIII, c.26. Participants: Cardinal Santacroce, Antonio Lomellino, Giovanni Antonio Zoni, Francesco Vannunzio, Angelo Massimo and Giacomo Crescenzi. The session served mainly to inform Santacroce of current commitments and requirements.

38   ASMP, '*Registri dei Decreti di Congregazione 1540–1566*', Tome 39, p.XIV, c.27. Santacroce did not attend. Bishop Scifola chaired the meeting. The other participants: Francesco Vannunzio, Angelo Massimo, Giovanni Antonio Zoni, Andrea Carillo, Bacco Giuntino, Giovanni Guadagni, Francesco Baccodi, Andrea Pelusi, Giovanni Maria de Tassi, Gian Giacomo Arrigoni , Diego Algezeiro and Lorenzo Virilio.

39   ASMP, '*Registri dei Decreti di Congregazione 1540–1566*', Tome 39, p.XV, c.29. Participants: Cardinal Carpi, Luigi de' Torres, Antonio Lomellino, Giovanni Antonio Zoni, Francesco Vannunzio, Lorenzo de' Castello, Lorenzo Virilio, Bishop Scifola, Bernardo de' Boni, Gian Pietro Crivelli, Andrea Pelusi, Andrea Carillo, Didaro Algezeiro, Gian Mario de' Tassi, Giovan Battista Tartaro, Giovanni Guadagni, Virgilio cantore S.O.N. pp., Vincenzo Margani, Giovan Battista Rossi and Gian Giacomo Calciati (perhaps a relative of Francesco, one of the founders of the Monte). Gian Piero Crivelli was elected *provvisore* to replace Angelo Massimo, who, the minutes show, had died before the meeting.

40   ASMP, '*Registri dei Decreti di Congregazione 1540–1566*', Tome 39, p.XIV, c.30 and c.31.32, respectively for the two meetings. Participants in the first: Luigi de' Torres, Antonio Lomellino, Giovanni Antonio Zoni, Lorenzo de' Castello, the bishop of Como, Gian Pietro Crivelli, Francesco Baccodi, Rocco de' Cenci, Gian Giacomo Tassi, Andrea Pelusi, Gian Mario de' Tassi, Giovan Battista Tartaro, Gerolamo Guadagni, Giacomo Arrigoni, Vincenzo Margani, Giovanni Nichelchim and Leonardo Pionati. Participants in the second: Cardinal Pio di Carpi, Filippo Archinto, Luigi de' Torres, Giovanni Arborino, Antonio Lomellino, Giovanni Antonio Zoni, Francesco Vannunzio, Bishop Scifola, the bishop of Como, Gian Piero Crivelli, Giovanni Battista Tartaro, Vincenzo Margani, Giovanni Battista, criminal court judge, Francesco Bonafede, Alamanno degli Alamanni, Gabriele de' Vallati and Andrea Bonturo.

41   ASMP, '*Registri di Brevi, Instromenti e Decreti di Congregazione, 1540–1604*', '*Nota Decretorum Congregationis 1540–1604*', p.2.

42   ASMP, '*Registri dei Decreti di Congregazione 1540–1566*', Tome 39, p.XVII, c.33. Participants: Cardinal Maffei, Giovanni Arborino, Giovanni Antonio Zoni, Bishop Scifola, Bernardo de' Boni, Giovanni Vincenzo Dolce, Gian Pietro Crivelli, Rocco de' Cenci, Agostino Pessina, Diego Algeziro, Giovanni Battista Tartaro, Giovanni and Gerolamo Guadagni, Vincenzo Margani and Pietro Francesco Fossani.

43   ASMP, '*Registri dei Decreti di Congregazione 1540–1566*', Tome 39, p.XVII, c.34, and p.XVII, c.35. Participants: Cardinal Maffei, Giovanni Arborino, Francesco Vannunzio, Bishop Scifola, Bernardo de' Boni, Gian Pietro Crivelli, Francesco Baccodi, Rocco de' Cenci, Agostino Pessina, Gian Giacomo Tassi, Andrea Pelusi, Diego Algeziro, Gian Mario de' Tassi, Giovanni Battista Tartaro, Giovanni and Gerolamo Guadagni, Vincenzo Margani, Gian Giacomo Arrigoni, Giovanni Nichelchim, Giovanni de' Vallati, Arcangelo Raimondi, Bernardino da Pescia, Giovanni Battista and Antonio Petri Mattei, Tiberio Margani, Pier Francesco Fossani, Flaminio de' Paoli, Alessandro Maroncelli, Franco Baruffi, Gabrio Porro, Gerolamo and Francesco Paparoni, Domenico Neri and Gerolamo Pirrotta.

44   See M. Tosi, *op. cit.*, pp.35–45.

45   The importance of this is testified to by the solemn mass celebrated on 20 August 1551 for the feast of Saint Bernard. See ASMP, '*Registri dei Decreti di Congregazione 1540–1566*', Tome 39, p.XVXII, c.36, Festività di San Bernardo. The mass was celebrated by Francesco Vannunzio.

46 ASMP, '*Registri dei Decreti di Congregazione 1540–1566*', Tome 39, p.XVIII, c.36, and p.XIX, c.37. Participants: Cardinal Carpi, the Bishop of Aquino (Pietro Vorsio), Giovanni Arborino, Antonio Lomellino, Francesco Vannunzio, Bishop Scifola, Bernardo de' Boni, Gian Pietro Crivelli, Giacomo Crescenzi, Agostino Pessina, Gian Giacomo Tassi, Andrea Pelusi, Diego Algeziro, Gian Maria de' Tassi, Giovanni Battista Tartaro, Gerolamo Guadagni, Vincenzo Margani, Alamanno degli Alamanni, Gabriele de' Vallati, Giovanni Battista and Antonio Petri Mattei, Alessandro Maroncelli, Valerio Valentino, Francesco Scibilia, Bernardino da Pescia, Arcangelo Raimondi and Alessandro Bartolini.

47 Under the new organisational chart, the four guardians had a narrower mandate and less authority than the two *provvisori* whom they replaced. Two were selected from among the delegates of the Monte (Antonio Lomellino, apostolic protonotary, and Bernardo de' Boni, the pope's personal referendary) and two from among those of the Company (Valerio Valentino and Antonio Petri Mattei). The functions of the accountant (keeping the books, preparing the 'financial statements' and inventories) were taken over by three delegates *pro indice*. Alamanno degli Alamanni was designated depositary general and Donato Bonsignore cashier; Gian Giacomo Tassi of the Monte and Alessandro Maroncelli of the Company of San Bernardo were named secretaries with the special function of attorneys.

48 Having a representative for each district amounted to covering the whole territory of the city. The decision must have stemmed from a desire to bring the Monte's operations closer to the real needs of its beneficiaries. It also was probably a legacy of the organisation of the Company of San Bernardo, which was much more highly ramified. The twelve assistants were: Latino de Mantarco (Pigna district), Gabriele de'Vallati (Sant'Angelo), Giovanni Milesi (Parione), Vincenzo Margani (Campitelli), Marcello Maroncelli (Trastevere), Andrea Pelusi (Ponte), Bernardino da Pescia (also Ponte), Alessandro Bartoli (Regola), Gian Pietro Cardelli (Campo Marzio), Gian Maria de Tassi (Trevi), Paolo de Giunove (Colonna) and Gian Maria Franco (Sant'Eustachio). Subsequently, there were usually thirteen (see the Statutes of 1581 attached).

49 ASMP, '*Registri dei Decreti di Congregazione 1540–1566*', Tome 39, p.XIX, c.38. Those attending: Antonio Lomellino, Bishop Scifola, Bernardo de' Boni, Arcangelo Raimondi, Giovanni Vincenzo Dolce, Francesco de Vaino, Gian Pietro Crivelli, Rocco de' Cenci, Agostino Pessina, Diego Algeziro, Gian Mario de Tassi, Giovanni Guadagni, Giovanni Battista Rossi, Giovanni Battista Petri Mattei, Antonio Albertoni, Alessandro Maroncelli, Gabrio Porro, Valerio Valentino and Alessandro Bartolini.

50 ASMP, '*Registri dei Decreti di Congregazione 1540–1566*', Tome 39, p.XX, c.39. Participants: Cardinal Pio di Carpi, Filippo Archinto, papal vicar for Rome, Bishop Scifola, Antonio Lomellino, apostolic protonotary, Giovanni Vincenzo Dolce, apostolic secretary, Bernardo de' Boni, papal referendary, Francesco Baccodi, notary and 'apostolic assistant', the Rev. Sig. Giovanni Battisti, assistant to the Vicar, Antonio Albertoni, Valerio Valentino, Rocco de' Cenci, Gian Pietro Crivelli, Bishop Virilio, Francesco Sibilla, Giovanni Battista Petri Mattei, Arcangelo Raimondi, Andrea Pelusi, Giovanni Nichelchim, Gerolamo Pirrotta, Diego (or Didaro) Algeziro and Agostino Pessina.

51 ASMP, '*Registri dei Decreti di Congregazione 1540–1566*', Tome 39, p.XX, c.40. The meeting was attended by Antonio Lomellino, Bernardo de' Boni, Francesco Vannunzio, Bacco Giuntino, Giacomo Crescenzi, Gerolamo Guadagni, Alessandro Barolini, Bishop Scifola of Mirandola, Lorenzo Virilio, Arcangelo Raimondi, Alamanno degli Alamanni, Francesco Bonafede, Giovanni Nichelchim, Diego Algeziro, Andrea Pelusi and Gian Giacomo Arrigoni. Archinto must have figured prominently in questions regarding credit. It is reported that he once received a group of rabbis to discuss the applicability for Jews of certain passages of Deuteronomy relating to lending and usury (B. Nelson, *op. cit.*, p.49).

52 ASMP, '*Registri dei Decreti di Congregazione 1540–1566*', Tome 39, p.XXI, c.41.

53 ASMP, '*Registri dei Decreti di Congregazione 1540–1566*', Tome 39, p.XXI, c.41–2. Participants: Cardinal Pio di Carpi, Filippo Archinto, Antonio Lomellino, Bishop Vincenzo Scifola, Fra Arcangelo Raimondi, Giacomo Crescenzi, Giambattista Rossi, Alessandro Bartoli(ni), Guardino de' Guardi, Giacomo Garburnio and Genesio Belsito.

54 ASMP, '*Registri dei Decreti di Congregazione 1540–1566*', Tome 39, pp.XXI–XXII, c.42–3. Participants: Cardinal Pio di Carpi, Filippo Archinto, Antonio Lomellino, Fra Arcangelo Raimondi, Vincenzo Dolce, Agostino Pessina, Diego (Didaro) Algeziro,

Giangiacomo Arrigoni, Giovambattista Rossi, Pietro Francesco Fossani, Alessandro Bartoli, Giacomo Garburnio, Genesio Belsito and Alfonso Diaz.

55 ASMP, '*Registri dei Decreti di Congregazione 1540–1566*', Tome 39, pp.XXII–XXIII, c.44–5. Participants: Cardinal Pio di Carpi, Agostino Pessina, Bernardino da Pescia, Alessandro Bartoli, Genesio Belsito and Alfonso Diaz. The transactions included a legacy of two emeralds to be appraised and acquired by the Monte, a legacy of money (800 *scudi*) bequeathed by the Genoese merchant Giovanni Battista Libardi, who had had business relations with the Monte, and a *fideicommissum* left by the late delegate of the congregation, Gian Maria de' Tassi. The legacy bequeathed by Libardi was especially interesting, given the latter's previous dealings with the Monte. Libardi's original will, dated 24 June 1548, must have included the instructions relating to this legacy (mentioned in ASMP, '*Registro di Lettere Apostoliche ed Instromenti Diversi*', c.71). Tosi (*op. cit.*, p.39) says he found traces of a cash deposit of 1000 *scudi* in the name of Libardi made at roughly the same period, with an explicit accord for payment of annual income of at least 100 *scudi*. This is a very telling case, since up to 1552 the Monte did not formally lend money at interest and was plagued by a chronic shortage of revenues.

56 Tosi, *op. cit.*, p.39.

57 ASMP, '*Registri dei Decreti di Congregazione 1540–1566*', Tome 39, pp.XXV, c.49–50. Participants: Cardinal Pio di Carpi, Antonio Lomellino, Bishop Vincenzo Scifola, Bishop Giacomo Jacomelli of Castrobello, Gerolamo Guadagni, Pietro Francesco Fossani, Alessandro Bartoli, Alfonso Diaz, Suardino Suardi, Luigi Chiappini and Giampietro Cardelli.

58 *Ibid.*

59 ASMP, '*Registri dei Decreti di Congregazione 1540–1566*', Tome 39, pp.XXVI, c.51. Participants: Cardinal Pio di Carpi, Bishop Giacomo Jacomelli, Bishop Vincenzo Scifola, Alfonso Diaz, Bernardo del Bene, Giovanni Battista Lomellino, Bernardino del Conte, Gian Giacomo Arrigoni, Diego Algeziro and Agostino Pessina.

60 ASMP, '*Registri dei Decreti di Congregazione 1540–1566*', Tome 39, pp.XXVI–XXVII, c.52–3. Participants: Bishop Vincenzo Scifola, Alfonso Diaz, Gerolamo Guadagni, Alessandro Bartolini and Bernardino del Conte.

61 ASMP, '*Registri dei Decreti di Congregazione 1540–1566*', Tome 39, pp.XXVIII, c.56. The minutes of this meeting were signed by Cardinal Rodolfo Pio di Carpi, Bishop Vincenzo Scifola, Alfonso Diaz, Alessandro Bartolini and Bernardino del Conte.

62 ASMP, Tome 13, '*Registri di Brevi, Instromenti e Decreti di Congregazione, 1540–1604*', section relative to the '*Nota Decretorum Congregationis 1540–1604*', references to 1557. The source explicitly refers to specific cases being reported in detail on folio 29 of the register of pledged assets (now lost).

63 *Ibid.*

64 *Ibid.*, references to 1563.

65 *Ibid.* The records do not mention the interest rate on the second loan.

66 During the meeting the seal of the Monte was officially handed over to the cashier. Subsequently, on 17 August, it was decided that the seal should be kept by the senior *provvisore*. This arrangement did not last, for on 27 June 1570 the congregation determined that the seal should be kept personally by the prelate of the Monte, who had the *provvisori* consign it to him. Another organisational measure was approved on 14 September 1568, when it was decided that the secretary of the Monte had to attend every meeting of the congregation. See ASMP, Tome 13, '*Registri di Brevi, Instromenti e Decreti di Congregazione, 1540–1604*', section relative to the '*Nota Decretorum Congregationis 1540–1604*', references to 1564–70.

67 *Ibid.*, references to 1571.

68 *Ibid.*

69 For example: '...and let 700 *scudi* be borrowed and 1050 repaid' (18 June), '...and let 100 *scudi* of an annuity be borrowed for 20 a year in order to extinguish another 100' (10 November 1567); '...offer of one to give 2000 luoghi del Monte in order to 10½ per cent a year during his lifetime, accepted' (8 February 1575). *Ibid.*, references to 1567 and 1575. On 1566 a loan of 1000 *scudi* at 8 per cent was obtained. *Ibid*, references to 1566.

70 *Ibid.*, references to 1569. On 11 October the congregation approved a freeze on the disbursement of loans and the return of collateral until Christmas. This was not due to financial trouble, since orders were given at the same time for the return of 'money held at interest'.

Notes to Appendix

71 On 14 August it decided to sell expired pledges from the previous year. A similar measure was adopted on 2 November 1565 for pledges expired in 1564 and 1565. On 26 October 1565 the congregation authorised a transaction involving a building with tenants against whom a legal action was pending. On 23 January 1565 the establishment of collection boxes in the city's churches had been proposed again, and four were authorised. *Ibid.*, references to 1564 and 1565.

72 *Ibid.*, references to 1567.

73 *Ibid.*, references to 1567 and 1570.

74 *Ibid.*, references to 1567.

75 *Ibid.*, references to 1571.

76 *Ibid.*, references to 1568.

77 Tosi maintains that this bull granted the Monte the authority of 'ordinary and perpetual judge' for disputes involving the Monte; M. Tosi, *op. cit.*, p.147.

78 ASMP, Tome 13, '*Registri di Brevi, Instromenti e Decreti di Congregazione, 1540–1604*', section relative to the '*Nota Decretorum Congregationis 1540–1604*', references to 1570. The dating of this text is not entirely certain. It could be a later version, perhaps the 'definitive' one attributable to the protectorate of Cardinal Pietro Aldobrandini (1602–21) or the printing ordered in 1581 by Filippo Guastavillani (protector from 1580 to 1587), but it could also be the text conserved in Vatican Codex 6203, pp.150–69. The debate on whether the so-called 'Statutes of Saint Charles' are the first official statutes of the Monte (excluding the 'brief' text of 1557) has been inconclusive. See D. Tamilia, *op. cit.*, and M. Tosi, *op. cit.*

79 It was decided that the cashier had to cover the expenses of running his office and he was granted 10 *scudi* as one-off reimbursement. On 13 January another meeting was held; it decided to invest the Monte's idle funds ('dead money') in the Monte della Carne.

80 ASMP, Tome 13, '*Registri di Brevi, Instromenti e Decreti di Congregazione, 1540–1604*', section relative to the '*Nota Decretorum Congregationis 1540–1604*', references to 1574.

81 This rule was modified several times. On 8 April 1578 the congregation ordered that neither officers nor salaried staff could buy on behalf of others, but could do so only in their own name and for own account. On 8 February and 15 March 1575 it established that congregations would be held after dinner during Lent and that 'lending and collection likewise is to take place after dinner, except on Monday morning'. On Monday collection was permissible until 'sermon time'. ASMP, Tome 13, '*Registri di Brevi, Instromenti e Decreti di Congregazione, 1540–1604*', section relative to the '*Nota Decretorum Congregationis 1540–1604*', references to 1575. The schedule was changed again on 31 October 1575, with all activities to be carried on every day and 'all employees to be on duty for five consecutive hours after sunrise, until the end of this coming April'. *Ibid.*

82 *Ibid.*

83 *Ibid.*

84 Alciati, scion of an ancient aristocratic family, was an influential prelate at the papal court. In addition to being protector of the Monte (and, presumably, of the Franciscans), he was Chamberlain of the College of Cardinals, and thus acting head of state during papal vacancies, and protector of the Order of Malta. He died in 1580.

85 Guastavillani's name sometimes appears as 'Vastavillano'. His personal history is recounted in *Serie Cronologica degli Eminentissimi e Reverendissimi Signori Cardinali Bolognesi compresi quelli assunti al sommo pontificato disposta secondo l'ordine del tempo dal giorno della loro esaltazione, ed avente il suo principio dall'anno 1060 fino al 1755 – Con l'epilogo della loro nascita, vita e morte, e rispetto ai viventi dei loro fatti fino al tempo corrente*, Bologna, Sassi, 1755, pp.32–3. Son of Angelo Michele of Bologna and Giacomo Boncompagni, the sister of Ugo (Pope Gregory XIII), Guastavillani was born in Bologna on 30 September 1540. Pius V named him to the Council of Forty in Bologna, where he headed the municipal administration. On 5 July 1573 his uncle appointed him cardinal-deacon of Santa Maria Nuova (he later assumed the title of Santa Maria in Cosmedin). Guastavillani served as protector of the Conventuals, of the city of Ancona, of the Order of Malta (succeeding Alciati), of the Rome Monte and of the Holy House of Loreto. He was also papal envoy in Bologna for the resolution of a dispute with the Duke of Ferrara and Chamberlain of the College of Cardinals. Guastavillani died in Rome on 6 August 1587. He was interred in the Church of Santi Apostoli, but in 1588 his body was removed and buried near the main altar of the church of the Conventuals in Bologna.

86 Tome 13, '*Registri di Brevi, Instromenti e Decreti di Congregazione, 1540–1604*', section relative to the '*Nota Decretorum Congregationis 1540–1604*', references to 1582.

87 This was notarised by an act of '*Not. Aug. Pinelli, 6 martii 1582*'; *ibid*. In the subsequent years other measures were taken regarding offices and personnel. On 27 March Monsignor Caetani was elected prelate of the Monte in place of Monsignor Fontana, who had left Rome. On 7 July 1582 Pietro Paulo Quartieri was appointed to succeeded Duttilio (Rutilio?) Strozzi as accountant. On 28 August 1582 a transaction with Gerolamo Prelario, cashier of the Monte, was authorised 'with an act of Gugnetti, notary'. On 25 September 1582 Agostino Giuntio was appointed custodian. On 6 December 1583 one Billa was elected cashier and Duttilio Strozzi re-elected accountant.

88 Tome 13, '*Registri di Brevi, Instromenti e Decreti di Congregazione, 1540–1604*', section relative to the '*Nota Decretorum Congregationis 1540–1604*', references to 1584.

89 *Ibid.*, references to 1581.

90 *Ibid.*, references to 1579.

91 The frontispiece of the official edition bears this date, which is most likely also the date the statutes entered into effect. Judging from the amendments the congregation adopted in January 1583, the 'final' version of the text was printed no later than early 1583.

BIBLIOGRAPHY

P. Abelard, 'Petri Abelardi Opera Theologica. Commentaria in Epistulam Pauli ad Romanos. Apologia contra Bernardum', in *Corpus Christianorum – continuatio mediaevalis*, 11, Turnhout, Buytaert, 1969

I. Ait, 'Credito e iniziativa commerciale: aspetti dell'attività economica a Roma nella seconda metà del XV secolo', *Atti del primo Convegno Nazionale (4–6 giugno 1987) della Società Italiana degli storici dell'economia su 'Credito e sviluppo economico in Italia dal Medio Evo all'Età Contemporanea'*, Verona, 1988, pp.67 ff.

P. Antonello, *Dalla pietà al credito – Il Monte di Pietà di Bologna fra Otto e Novecento*, Bologna, Il Mulino, 1997

A. Antoniazzi Villa, *Un processo contro gli ebrei nella Milano del 1488. Crescita e declino della comunità ebraica lombarda alla fine del Medioevo*, Bologna, Il Mulino, 1986

Anonymous, *Il vero stato degli Ebrei in Roma*, Rome, Stamperia del Varese, 1668

Anonymous, *Serie Cronologica degli Eminentissimi e Reverendissimi Signori Cardinali Bolognesi compresi quelli assunti al sommo pontificato disposta secondo l'ordine del tempo dal giorno della loro esaltazione, ed avente il suo principio dall'anno 1060 fino al 1755 – Con l'epilogo della loro nascita, vita e morte, e rispetto ai viventi dei loro fatti fino al tempo corrente*, Bologna, Sassi, 1755

Thomas Aquinas, *Summa Theologiae* (vols. IV–XVII of *Opera Omnia*, Rome, 1882); Alexander of Hales, *Summa Theologica*, Florence, Quaracchi, 1924

F. Arcelli, 'A Banking Enterprise at the Papal Court: the Company of Antonio Della Casa and Jacopo di Michele di Corso Donati 1438–1440', *The Journal of European Economic History*, vol. 25, no. 1 (Spring 1996), pp.9–32

F. Arcelli, 'La costituzione della compagnia di Antonio della Casa e Jacopo di Michele di Corso Donati presso la corte pontificia (1438–1440)', *Studi Romani*, vol. XLV, no. 1–2 (Jan.–June 1997), pp.5–26

F. Arcelli, 'Quando i vincoli creano l'innovazione: un parallelo storico', *Confronto*, no. 1 (Jan.–June 1997)

F. Arcelli, *Gli Statuti del 1581 del Sacro Monte di Pietà di Roma*, Soveria Mannelli (CZ), Rubbettino, 1999

M.F. Barry, *The Vocabulary of the Moral-Ascetical Works of Saint Ambrose. A Study in Latin Lexicography*, Washington, The Catholic University of America, 1926

Saint Bernardine of Siena, *Quadragesimale de Christiana Religione, Opera II*, Florence, Quaracchi, 1950

M. Blaugh, *Storia e critica della dottrina economica*, Turin, Boringhieri, 1970

S. Bonaventura da Bagnoregio, *Opera Omnia*, Florence, Quaracchi, 1882 and subsequent years

V. Bonazzoli, 'Monti di Pietà e politica economica delle città delle Marche alla fine del "400", in *Banchi pubblici, banchi privati e monti di pietà nell'Europa preindustriale*, Proceedings of the conference held in Genoa, 1–6 October 1990, Genoa, Società Ligure di Storia Patria, 1991

F. Braudel, *The Mediterranean and the Mediterranean World in the Age of Philip II*, New York, Harper & Row, 1972; second revised edition

F. Braudel, *La dinamica del capitalismo*, Bologna, Il Mulino, 1977

O. Capitani, *Storia dell'Italia Medievale (410–1216)*, Bari, Laterza, 1986

O. Capitani (ed.), *Una economia politica nel Medioevo*, Bologna, Pàtron, 1987

M. Carboni, *Il debito della città – Mercato del credito, fisco e società a Bologna fra Cinque e seicento*, Bologna, Il Mulino, 1995

M. Carta, *Il Palazzo del Monte di Pietà di Roma*, in the series 'I palazzi della Banca di Roma', Rome, Arti grafiche f.lli Palombi, 1994

M. Cassandro, *Il libro giallo di Ginevra della compagnia fiorentina di Antonio della Casa e Simone Guadagni, 1453–1454*, Prato, Istituto Internazionale di Storia Economica F. Datini, 1976

M. Cassandro, 'Sulla storia economica degli Ebrei nei secoli XV–XVII. Problemi, orientamenti e prospettive', in *Studi in memoria di Mario Abrate*, Turin, 1986

M. Cattini, 'L'economia rurale in epoca preindustriale – proposta di un modello interpretativo', in *Dall'età preindustriale all'età del capitalismo*, Parma, Studi e ricerche dell'Università deglio Studi di Parma, 1977

M. Cattini, 'Problemi di liquidità e prestito ad interesse nelle campagne emiliane – Secoli XVI–XVII', *Studi Storici L. Simeoni*, XXXIII (1983)

M. Ciardini, *I banchieri ebrei in Firenze nel secolo XV e il monte di pietà fondato da Girolamo Savonarola – Appunti di storia economica con appendice di documenti*, Borgo San Lorenzo, 1907; reprinted Florence, 1970, doc. VI

C.M. Cipolla, *Storia economica dell'Europa preindustriale*, Bologna, Il Mulino, 1974

C.M. Cipolla, 'Il governo della moneta a Firenze e a Milano nei secoli XIV–XVI', in *La repubblica internazionale del denaro*, edited by A. De Maddalena and H. Kellenbenz, Bologna, Il Mulino, 1986

F. Colzi, 'I Monti del popolo romano', doctoral dissertation, VIII ciclo, Università degli Studi di Bari

A. Cova, 'Banchi e monti pubblici in Milano nei secoli XVI e XVII', in *Banchi pubblici, banchi privati e monti di pietà nell'Europa preindustriale*, Proceedings of the conference held in Genoa, 1–6 October 1990, Genoa, Società Ligure di Storia Patria, 1991

R. de Roover, *Money, Banking, and Credit in Mediaeval Bruges: Italian Merchant-Bankers, Lombards, and Money-Changers*, Cambridge, Mass., The Mediaeval Academy of America, 1948

R. de Roover, 'The Concept of the Just Price', *Journal of Economic History*, 18 (1958), pp.539–66

R. de Roover, *The Rise and Decline of the Medici Bank, 1397–1494*, Cambridge, Mass., Harvard University Press, 1963; reprinted New York, Norton, 1966

L. De Rosa, 'Banchi pubblici, banchi privati e monti di pietà a Napoli nei secoli XVI e XVIII', in *Banchi pubblici, banchi privati e monti di pietà nell'Europa preindustriale*, Proceedings of the conference held in Genoa, 1–6 October 1990, Genoa, Società Ligure di Storia Patria, 1991

L. De Rosa, 'Storia della Banca e della Borsa', in *Dizionario di Banca, Borsa e Finanza*, Rome, Ipsoa, 1993

J. Delumeau, *Vie économique et sociale de Rome dans la seconde moitié du XVI siècle*, Paris, 1957–9, two vols.

G. Duby, *L'economia rurale nell'Europa Medievale*, Bari, Laterza, 1970

Pietro di Tarantasia, 'Quodlibet', *Revue de Théologie ancienne et médiévale*, Paris, Glorieux, 1937

A. Esch, 'La fine del libero comune di Roma nel giudizio dei mercanti fiorentini. Lettere romane degli anni 1395–1398 nell'Archivio Datini', *Bollettino dell'Istituto Storico Italiano per il Medio Evo*, 1976–7, pp.235–77

L. Falchi, 'Sisto V e l'Annona: l'eredità di un secolo', *Dimensioni e problemi della ricerca storica*, 1990, no. 2, pp.91–108

A. Fanfani, *Storia Economica. Parte I, Antichità – Medioevo – Età Moderna*, Turin, UTET, 1968

C. Fanucci, *Trattato di tutte le Opere pie dell'alma città di Roma*, Rome, Stampatori Lepido Facili e Stefano Paolini, 1602

J. Favier, *Les finances pontificales a l'époque du Grand Schisme d'Occident (1378–1409)*, Paris, Boccard – Bibliothéque des écoles françaises d'Athènes et de Rome, no. 211

M. Fornasari, 'Il Monte di Pietà di Ravenna: storia di una istituzione sociale (1492–1939)', in M. Fornasari, P. Mita and M. Poli, *I cinquecento anni del Monte di Ravenna (1492–1992)*, Bologna, Il Mulino, 1992, published on behalf of the Fondazione del Monte di Bologna e Ravenna

M. Fornasari, *Il Thesoro della città – Il Monte di Pietà e l'economia bolognese nei secoli XV ed XVI*, Bologna, Il Mulino, 1993, published in the series on economic and banking history, promoted by the Fondazione del Monte di Bologna e Ravenna

Jan A. Goris, *Etudes sur les colonies marchandes méridionales a Anvers de 1488 à 1567*, Louvain, 1925

F. Gregorovius, *History of the City of Rome in the Middle Ages* (Italian translation: *Storia della città di Roma nel Medioevo*, Rome, 1901)

A. Grohmann, 'Credito ed economia urbana nel basso Medioevo', in *Atti del primo Convegno Nazionale (4–6 giugno 1987) della Società Italiana degli storici dell'economia su 'Credito e sviluppo economico in Italia dal Medioevo all'Età Contemporanea'*, Verona, 1988

J. Hamesse (ed.), *Thesaurus Librorum Sententiarum Petrii Lombardi*, Louvain-la-Neuve, Cetedoc, 1991

D. Herlihy and C. Klapisch-Zuber, *Tuscans and Their Families: a Study of the Florentine Catasto of 1427*, Yale University Press, 1985 (Italian edition, 'I toscani e le loro famiglie. Uno studio sul catasto fiorentino del 1427', 1988)

Hincmar, Archbishop of Rheims (845–882), 'De ordine palatii,' in *Monumenta Germaniae Historica*, 3, Hannover, Gross-Schieffer, 1980

J.M. Keynes, *The General Theory of Employment, Interest and Money*, New York, St. Martin's Press, 1961

R.M. Kidd, 'Wealth and beneficence in the Pastor. Epistles: An Inquiry into a "Bourgeois" Form of Early Christianity', Dissertation at Duke University, Durham, NC, 1990

J.M. Kulischer, *Storia economica del Medio Evo e dell'epoca moderna*, Florence, Sansoni, 1964, vol. II

Henry S. Lucas, *Medieval Economic Relations between Flanders and Greenland*, vol. 12, 1937, pp.167–81

M. Luzzati, 'Ruolo e funzioni dei banchi ebraici dell'Italia centro-settentrionale nei secoli XV e XVI', in *Banchi pubblici, banchi privati e monti di pietà nell'Europa preindustriale*, Proceedings of the conference held in Genoa, 1–6 October 1990, Genoa, Società Ligure di Storia Patria, 1991

C. Manca, *L'economia mercantile marittima*, Padua, CEDAM, 1995

F. Melis, 'Industria, Commercio, Credito', in *Un'altra Firenze*, Florence, 1971

F. Melis, *Documenti per la storia economica dei secoli XIII–XVI*, Florence, Leo S. Olschki, 1972

F. Melis, 'La grande conquista trecentesca del "credito di esercizio" e la tipologia dei suoi strumenti fino al XVI secolo', reprinted in A. Vannini Marx (ed.), *Credito, banche e investimenti (secolo XIII–XX)*, Florence, Le Monnier, 1985

G. Mira, 'Considerazioni sulla lotta dei Monti di Pietà contro il prestito ebraico', in *Scritti in memoria di Sally Mayer*, Milan, 1956

G. Mira, 'Note sul Monte di Pietà di Perugia dalle origini alla seconda metà del XVI secolo', in *Archivi storici delle aziende di credito*, Rome, ABI – Associazione Bancaria Italiana, 1956

J. Mossay (ed.), *Thesaurus Sancti Gregorii Nazianzeni (Orationes, Epistolae, Testamentum)*, Louvain-la-Neuve, Cetedoc, 1990

M.G. Muzzarelli, *Banchi ebraici a Bologna nel XV secolo*, Bologna, Il Mulino, 1994

B. Nelson, *Usura e Cristianesimo. Per una storia della genesi dell'etica moderna*, Florence, Sansoni, 1967

Origene, *In Matthaeum (versio latina antiqua)*, Berlin, Klostermann-Benz, 1935 and subsequent years

L. Palermo, 'Ricchezza privata e debito pubblico nello Stato della Chiesa durante il XVI secolo', *Studi Romani*, vol. XXII, no. 3 (Jul.–Sep. 1974)

L. Palermo, 'L'anno santo dei mercanti: dibattito storiografico e documenti economici sul cosiddetto giubileo del 1400', in *Studi in onore di Paolo Brezzi*, Rome, 1988

L. von Pastor, *History of the Popes from the Close of the Middle Ages*, various editions (Italian translation: *Storia dei Papi dalla fine del Medio Evo compilata col sussidio dell'Archivio Segreto Pontificio e di molti altri Archivi*, Rome, Desclee & Ci., 1950–65)

F. Piola Caselli, 'Aspetti del debito pubblico nello Stato Pontificio: gli uffici vacabili', *Annali della facoltà di scienze politiche dell'Università degli studi di Perugia*, 1970–1972

F. Piola Caselli, 'La diffusione dei luoghi di monte della Camera Apostolica alla fine del XVI secolo', in *Atti del primo Convegno Nazionale (4–6 giugno 1987) della Società Italiana degli storici dell'economia su 'Credito e sviluppo economico in Italia dal Medioevo all'Età Contemporanea'*, Verona, 1988

F. Pisa, 'Attività bancarie locali nell'Italia dei secoli XIV–XVI', *Zakhor – rivista di storia degli ebrei d'Italia – Mercanti e banchieri ebrei*, no. 1, 1997

L. Poliakov, *Les banquiers Juifs e le Saint-Siège du XIII au XVII siècle*, Paris, 1967

P. Prodi, *Il Sovrano Pontefice. Un corpo e due anime: la monarchia papale nella prima età moderna*, Bologna, Il Mulino, 1982

P. Prodi, 'La nascita dei Monti di Pietà: tra solidarismo cristiano e logica del profitto', *Annali dell'Istituto Italo-Germanico*, VII, Trento, 1982

M.A. Romani, 'La carestia del 1590–93 nei ducati padani: crisis congiunturale e/o di struttura', in *Studi in onore di Gino Barbieri*, Salerno, IPEM, 1983

J.A. Schumpeter, *The Theory of Economic Development. An Inquiry into Profits, Capital, Credit, Interest and the Business Cycle*, New York, Oxford University Press, 1961

S. Simonsohn, 'Lo stato attuale della ricerca storica sugli ebrei in Italia', in *Italia Judaica I*, Proceedings of the first international conference held in Bari on 18–22 May 1981, Rome, 1983

S. Simonsohn, *The Apostolic See and the Jews (1492–1555), Documents and History*, Toronto, 1988–91

D. Tamilia, *Il Sacro Monte di Pietà di Roma*, Rome, Forzani, 1900

A. Tenenti, 'Un primo bilancio', in *Gli ebrei e Venezia (secoli XIV–XVIII)*, Proceedings of the international conference organised by the Istituto di storia della società e dello stato veneziano della Fondazione Giorgio Cini, Venice, 5–10 June 1983, edited by G. Cozzi and R. Bonfil, Milan, 1987

G. Todeschini, 'Gli ebrei medioevali come minoranza attiva nella storiografia italiana degli ultimi trent'anni', in *La storia degli ebrei nell'Italia medioevale: tra filologia e metodologia*, Bologna, Istituto per i beni artistici e culturali della regione Emilia-Romagna, 1990

G. Todeschini, *Il prezzo della salvezza – Lessici medievali del pensiero economico*, Rome, Nuova Italia Scientifica, 1993

M. Tosi, *Il Sacro Monte di Pietà di Roma e le sue Amministrazioni*, Rome, Ist. Pol. dello Stato, 1936

C.M. Travaglini, 'Le Origini del Banco dei Depositi del Monte di Pietà di Roma e le prime emissioni di cedole (secc. XVI–XVII)', *Atti del Secondo Convegno Nazionale della Società Italiana degli Storici dell'Economia (4–6 March 1993)*, Bologna, Monduzzi, 1996

L. Vereeke, *Da Guglielmo di Ockham a Sant'Alfonso de' Liguori. Saggi di storia della teologia morale moderna (1300–1787)*, Milan, Edizioni Paoline, 1990

L. Wadding, *Annales Minorum*

M. Weber, *The Protestant Ethic and the Spirit of Capitalism*, London, Routledge, 1985

ARCHIVE REFERENCES

Archivio del Sacro Monte di Pietà di Roma, in Banca di Roma SpA Archives

'Registro di Bolle, Brevi e Decreti di Congregazione', Tome I, 'Ad Sacram Beati Petri Sedem' (bulla, 1539)

'Nota Decretorum Congregationis Sacri Montis Pietatis ab initio erectionis dicti Montis usque in praesentem diem (1540–1604)', in 'Registri di Brevi, Istromenti e Decreti di Congregazione del S. Monte di Pietà dal 1540 al 1604 o meglio al 1626', Tome 13

'Registri dei Decreti di Congregazione del Sacro Monte di Pietà di Roma (1540–1566)', Tome 39

'Registri dei Decreti di Congregazione del Sacro Monte di Pietà di Roma (1566–1579)', Tome 40

'Registri dei Decreti di Congregazione del Sacro Monte di Pietà di Roma (1580–1593)', Tome 41

'Registri dei Decreti di Congregazione del Sacro Monte di Pietà di Roma (1633–1643)', Tome 45

'Nota di libri e scritture che si trovano nell'archivio del Sacro Monte della Pietà, et appresso li officiali et ministri di detto Monte reviste et poste per ordine de' tempi dal Sig. Carlo Gabrielli, Deputato, come per decreto a dì 13 di Maggio 1603', Tome 258

'Inventario de libri e scritture del Sacro Monte di Pietà dal 1539 al 1634', Tome 278

'Registri de' Provvisori del Sacro Monte di Pietà di Roma dal 1575 al 1579', Tome 306

Archivio Segreto Vaticano

'Bolle per diverse Militie di Cavalieri per diversi collegij di Roma per il Monte di Pietà e per la S.ta Casa di Loreto', Armario IV, Tome 22, pp.486–506 (statutes of 1581)

'Bolle per diverse Militie di Cavalieri per diversi collegij di Roma per il Monte di Pietà e per la S.ta Casa di Loreto', Armario IV, Tome 22, pp.483–5, 507–17

Archivio di Stato di Roma

'Libri Mastri di Conto del Sacro Monte di Pietà di Roma', Ledger I (1584–5)